AND STILL
RICKY VILLA

To my mother and father, my wife Cristina, and to my children Maria Eugenia, Martina, Mariana and Ricky

AND STILL
RICKY VILLA

MY AUTOBIOGRAPHY with Joel Miller
& Federico Ardiles

VSP

Published by Vision Sports Publishing in 2010

Vision Sports Publishing
19–23 High Street
Kingston upon Thames
Surrey
KT1 1LL

www.visionsp.co.uk

ISBN 13: 978-1905326-89-1

Editor: Jim Drewett
Design: Doug Cheeseman
Copy editing: Ian Turner, John Murray
Front cover images: Colorsport
Back cover image: Getty Images/Bob Thomas

Typeset by Palimpsest Book Production Limited, Falkirk, Stirlingshire

Printed and bound in the UK by CPI Mackays, Chatham ME5 8TD

Mixed Sources
Product group from well-managed
forests and other controlled sources
www.fsc.org Cert no. SGS-COC-004081
FSC © 1996 Forest Stewardship Council

CONTENTS

Foreword by
OSSIE ARDILES

I could tell within the first two minutes of any game whether Ricky was about to play well or not. That's all it took. He was an incredibly talented footballer but so wildly inconsistent. There were occasions when I saw him produce performances of which Diego Maradona would have been proud; on other days, however, he was completely different. So different, in fact, that if I hadn't known him and someone had told me, "That guy is a professional footballer" then I would have said, "No chance!" There was no middle ground.

But that's Ricky. That's his nature. And I should know, of course. More than 35 years have passed since we first met, an eventful passage of time during which we embarked on an extraordinary journey together: an unforgettable, life-changing experience. Side by side we took on the toughest of challenges and, as the closest of friends, we came through them all.

Not that we hit it off immediately. In February 1975 Argentina's national team manager, César Luis Menotti, introduced the *Selección del Interior*, a squad consisting of players based outside Buenos Aires. It allowed Menotti to have a closer look at those who weren't associated with the capital's big clubs, and Ricky and

I – as two young stars in the ascendancy – were both selected. To begin with we were effectively rivals rather than friends – Menotti played him in my position! That only lasted for one or two practice games, though, before Ricky was afforded a 'free' role behind the strikers and I was deployed on the right side of midfield.

It was not until the build-up to the 1978 World Cup that I became good friends with Ricky. It was then, as roommates at our training camp, that we developed a strong connection. Mario Kempes also stayed in our room: Me, Ricky and Mario – the three musketeers! Because of the pressure we were under as a team at that time it was so important to share the strain with those around us, to talk about the high demands and to discuss any general concerns. As a result, we formed an incredible bond.

I can't say we're similar characters though. Ricky was so much more relaxed when it came to football, almost to the point of looking uninterested at times. He never thought too much about the game, rarely asked questions and didn't really worry about his performances. His game was all about inspiration. Ricky was a spontaneous, instinctive player. He was fantastically gifted. In England he didn't understand the teamtalks for a while – even though he pretended to listen – but that was irrelevant really. Ricky wasn't a player who needed instructions. He was a free spirit. I didn't have a clue how he was going to perform from one game to the next, which was frustrating for me. Sometimes I felt like shaking him, he was so laid back. I tried to gee him up before the big games. I used to nudge him and say, "Come on Ricky, this is a huge match." I did my best to motivate him. He just nodded and said, "OK." That was it! After a while I gave up. Ricky was an enigma. But somehow the other players in our team understood that and he was regarded with great affection.

FOREWORD

Ricky and I were already great companions before we moved to England; afterwards we became like brothers. We lived next door to each other, we ate dinner with our families together, we spoke over the garden fence – we spoke all the time – we travelled to training in the same car and we shared a room on away trips.

I loved life in England from the very beginning, but for Ricky it was a different matter. I found it easier to adapt. I spoke a little English and I was eager to learn more. More so than Ricky, I would say, and that's where his problems were rooted. Ricky found it difficult to have conversations with people. To appreciate the effect this had on him you must first understand Ricky's personality. Believe me, Ricky loves to talk. He could talk for the championship of the world. So being incapable of fully expressing himself to people, or to make a joke, was incredibly frustrating for him. He couldn't be himself in that respect. By telling his story now he has given people in England an opportunity to appreciate the type of character he is.

I was often Ricky's translator. Sometimes my translation wasn't completely accurate, though. There was one television interview when the reporter asked a question which I translated to Ricky. I can't remember exactly what the question was – maybe something like, "Has it been difficult settling into English football?" Ricky's reply – in Spanish – went on for some time. As I've already mentioned, when speaking in his native tongue there is no stopping Ricky. He could chat all day. I waited patiently while he constructed a detailed response, and when he finally finished talking I turned to the reporter. "Yes," I answered. Simple!

In terms of the football we were targeted at first, definitely. When we received the ball we could afford to have no more than one or two touches before releasing it. If we held on to it for any longer than that we would get clobbered. Opponents used to talk a lot as well, stuff like, "Take me on and I'll break your leg." That soon got pretty boring, and was all quite ineffective really – the threats never bothered me, while Ricky couldn't understand a word of them anyway! Somehow I found it easier to get on the ball than Ricky. Most teams in England played 4-4-2 and the 'number 10' role that Ricky revelled in didn't really exist as we knew it. We had to invent a position for him. We must have done something right, though, because we stuck around for longer than many predicted; some said we wouldn't survive the first winter. We did survive, and we're still regarded as a double act to this day. No matter where I am, the first question people seem to ask me is, "How's Ricky?" Or, "Where's your other half?" That makes us sound like a married couple. We aren't like a married couple though – we've never argued! Not even once. Believe me, it's impossible to argue with Ricky.

Our adventure began so long ago now but I can still vividly remember how it came about. The president of my club in Argentina, Huracán, called me to say that a guy from England wanted me to play for his team and that the two clubs had already reached an agreement. I was interested straight away. When I was asked to suggest another player to accompany me I immediately thought of Ricky. First of all because he was my friend, but also because with his ability I was sure he could make an impact in English football. I could never have predicted just how big an impact, of course. I'm just glad he agreed to join me, and I know Tottenham fans are too. My 'other half' has quite a tale to tell.

Ossie Ardiles
October 2010

PROLOGUE

All I ever wanted to do was score a special goal.

Before every single match, in dressing rooms from Buenos Aires to Bristol City, from the Nou Camp to Old Trafford, and from Montevideo to Meadow Lane, I always contemplated just one thing as I sat quietly among fidgety teammates and considered what fortunes the ensuing 90 minutes would bring.

All I could think about was illuminating the occasion with a moment of brilliance, a moment that would lift the crowd from their seats and generate a round of applause, a moment they would never forget. That was my motivation.

And then it happened; I scored a special goal and things were never quite the same again.

The grandest of stages, a television audience of millions, a vibrant stadium bulging to capacity and a scent of glory in the air.

It had been such a close game, such an evenly contested encounter, that the mixture of excitement and apprehension emanating from the stands was thrilling. The next goal was sure to be decisive, and I was to claim it. This was the moment I'd been craving.

It happened so quickly but I can still recall every detail of the move, every touch, feint and swerve. I found myself in possession of the ball some 30 yards from goal. At first, it was not an obvious opportunity to score, but as I tricked my way beyond three defenders I was suddenly confronted with an inviting path to goal, and a growing hum of anticipation from the terraces confirmed my sense of a crucial opening.

The small matter of beating the last line of defence – an imposing goalkeeper rushing from his line in a final attempt to halt my progress – was still to be negotiated.

The keeper's efforts were, however, in vain, because this was my special goal. I found a finish to match the daring approach, and my frenzied run of celebration was accompanied by an almighty roar that engulfed the stadium. The sensation that followed for a brief period was one of numbing elation, an intense surge of joy that I thought I'd never experience again.

But you've probably heard all this before. Or maybe not.

It was October 1973, and I had just scored the greatest goal of my life against the famous River Plate. Suddenly, everyone knew who Ricardo Villa was.

Chapter One
LA PELOTA

Looking back, I still wonder how I ever made it as a *futbolista*.

It should never have happened really, because if there is such a thing as a conventional route to the top of the professional game then I certainly didn't take it. Far from it. Boys raised on a farm in the remote surroundings of Argentina's Pampas just don't go on to win the World Cup, or score a beautiful goal at Wembley. The fact that I did, I think, makes mine an interesting story to tell.

I grew up in the countryside – *el campo* – in a small house made of mud-brick. Our home was typical of the sort inhabited by *gaucho* families such as ourselves. A simple structure built on an iron frame, the house was encircled by a cluster of trees that provided much-needed shade from the scorching sun. Our house could definitely be described as 'detached'. Detached from almost everyone and everything, in fact. With a vast expanse of flat land all around us, on a clear day you could just about see . . . a vast expanse of flat land. Standing outside our home, even the nearest house was undetectable to the naked eye. Our closest 'neighbours' lived more than a mile away.

Roque Pérez is my home. A large farming community situated 130 kilometres south of Buenos Aires, it's where I live now – along with approximately 11,000 other residents – and it's where I'll always stay. I'm lucky in that my career afforded me the enlightening experience of living in a variety of places – England, the USA and Colombia, as well as an assortment of locations in Argentina. But, wherever I've been, an instinctive draw towards home has never left me.

Right now I live in the main town, and have done since 1990. As a child though, a distance of roughly 15 kilometres separated our house from that town. Without a car, or a bike, or the option of taking a bus – we were too far out of range for that to be a consideration – that 15-kilometre stretch of dirt track may as well have been a million miles long. That's how it felt at times anyway.

The horse was our primary mode of transport. Seriously. I rode mine to school every day, five kilometres there and five kilometres back, from the age of six until I was 12. That might sound odd to some people now, but to me it was just the way we lived. Most kids learn how to ride a bike during infancy. I learned how to ride a horse before I was six years old.

My strong sense of belonging to home is, I think, rooted in my ancestry. By the time I made my grand entrance into the world, on 18th August 1952, the Villa family had long been settled in *el campo*. My great-grandfather was Spanish, hailing from the northern region of Cantabria, and he was among a massive wave of immigrants that flooded into Argentina from Spain during the late 19th and early 20th centuries. Millions came to Argentina – a former Spanish colony – in search of fertile land and a more prosperous future.

My great-grandfather set up home as a farmer in Roque Pérez. His Argentinian-born son Pablo followed suit, and in 1921 Pablo's wife Rosa gave birth to Pedro Julio Villa – my father. He continued the family tradition which I have maintained to this day – I harvest crops and own a large herd of cattle – so the Villa family have been farming this land for more than 100 years. What a history! And we're still going strong, with my son, Ricky Jr, helping me out now.

It's not just Spain where my heritage is rooted. My grandmother Rosa was born in France – I can remember her serenading us with renditions of the French national anthem *La Marseillaise* – while, on my mother's side of the family, my grandfather was born in Venice. So that means there is a little bit of Argentina, Spain, France and Italy in me. I have always regarded myself as a Spanish-Argentine though. I mean that in a cultural sense – I like the food and the music. Villa is a typically Spanish name. And, obviously, we share the same language. I tell my wife Cristina that I'm definitely not Italian. "I'm not sure about those Italian people," I say to her. "They're always shouting at each other." I don't mean it, of course. I'm only teasing – I say it because her family originate from Italy.

My father Pedro, one of eight children, was a *peón*. A *peón* is a low-paid labourer who does not own the land he farms on. *Peóns* like my father rent plots of land and earn a living by selling the produce. Many other *peóns* lived and worked across the mass of land surrounding Roque Pérez. We certainly weren't alone in that respect. I would estimate that around 100 other families like the Villas can trace their roots in the area back through several generations. In addition – on a much higher level, in terms of status – there are maybe 10 super-rich families who own huge areas of the land, thanks to their Spanish forefathers attaining authority some centuries ago.

We all did our bit around the farm – my father, my mother, me, and my sister Noemí. (My only sibling, Noemí is two years older than me.) I was only 12 when I finished my formal education. The five-kilometre journey on horseback through the fields to primary school – where I was joined by 26 other pupils who appeared from all corners of the region, including five in my year group – was one thing. Attending secondary school, however, was another challenge altogether. It just wasn't viable, either logistically – it was too far to travel – or financially – my parents couldn't afford to cover the costs involved. So, once I left primary school, I assisted my father on the farm instead.

I was restricted in what I could do because of my age, but I still mucked in. Every morning I milked the cows, and also made sure they were properly penned in. I dug up potatoes and carrots, and picked tomatoes. I was shown how to kill chickens – hold the legs tight in one hand and tug the neck with the other. I accompanied my father when he went out shooting pheasant and hares. Not that I was much of a hunter. Too young to handle a real weapon, I was given a small pellet gun. It was a toy really. The only way I could have seriously harmed a small animal was if I'd asked it to sit still for a few minutes while I fired off several rounds from close range. So I was very much an observer on those excursions.

My diet as a child was excellent. I ate lots of chicken, eggs and ham, all full of protein. I was a strong boy. I had a great childhood, even though the living conditions were modest to say the least. We had no electricity, and the dirt base of our house wasn't covered – my mother used to spray the floor with water, to dampen it and prevent clouds of dust forming. We had an old tin bath, although that was only used in the summer; it was too cold in the winter months, when a quick wash had to suffice. As for the toilet, that was outside. It was a small enclosed cubicle that was tidy, hygienic and comfortable enough. Certainly more sophisticated than a simple hole in the ground. No one relished paying a visit when the rain came down though, or when it was freezing cold in the winter.

I can honestly say that I was never bored as a kid, and that was all because of one thing – football. As pastimes go, where I come from there really was only football. Especially when your father loved the game as mine did. He played in a local league until he broke a leg at the age of 20. It's funny when you compare the two of us as footballers. My father was a defender, particularly quick and a useful marker. I was an attacker, particularly slow and never the least bit interested in defending. How could that have happened? We were complete opposites on a football pitch. Fused together we would have made the perfect player.

My father instilled in me a strong sense of self-belief. He was a clever man who enjoyed reading, taking an interest in both historical events and current affairs, and was a keen conversationalist. He was a placid, easy-going character who went through life with a smile on his face. It wasn't from him, then, that I inherited my competitive spirit. That came from my mother. Maybe it's because of her Italian roots, I don't know, but my mother possessed a certain edge that was mirrored in my own personality. She followed football. She could see how happy I was when I had a ball at my feet so she encouraged me to practise. "Do something special on the pitch," she used to tell me. It was an ethos I maintained throughout my career.

I remember so clearly the first time my father brought me home a proper football, when I was six or seven years old. It was magical. A dark yellow/brownish leather football that I did not let out of my sight. I can almost smell that leather now. I didn't use it for the first three days that it was in my possession. I just slept with it.

As a child, all I ever thought about was football. I wanted to be a professional footballer and, with some clarity, I had a vision of what was required in order to fulfil my dream. I practised for hours. And then I practised even more. Nobody taught me specific techniques or gave me particular exercises to do. My father would join me at the end of the day, but he was always so tired after a hard day's work that his participation was only fleeting. Due to the remote location of our house I had no friends nearby to play with. No matter – the football was my friend! I had no option but to practise alone. My playing area was a dusty patch of ground outside the house. Wearing sandal-like *alpargatas* I set about mastering all the basics, practising with different parts of both feet and doing thousands of keep-ups. I would think up a specific skill and dedicate my time solely to perfecting it. When I'd accomplished that, after ten days or so, I would practise something else. I also incorporated the surroundings into my regime. I spent long periods passing the ball against the wall – again, using both feet – knocking it back and forth, back and forth. I even used the trees as imaginary defenders so that I could improve my dribbling technique; little did I know it at the time, but that drill laid the foundations for the most celebrated moment of my life.

Looking back, I would estimate that I spent between three or four hours outside with my football every day. The only time I went indoors was to sleep, or if it was raining. That ball used to get so heavy when it was wet; heading it was painful, and I think that goes a long way to explaining why I was never renowned for my aerial prowess. Come to think of it, I didn't enjoy heading the ball in any weather conditions.

Although football occupied most of my time as a youngster, there are plenty of other events that I can recall from my childhood, like taking a trip into town every two or three weeks to buy clothes or other necessities. I used to ride in on a horse-drawn *sulqui*, which is essentially a wooden seat with a big wheel on either side, similar to a horse and cart. I also remember listening to records on our wind-up gramophone. It was one of those classic models with a big horn attached. When it broke, my sister and I still tried to play the music, by spinning the records with our fingers. Getting the speed of the rotations correct on such occasions is no easy skill. I wish I'd kept hold of that gramophone, purely for sentimental reasons, which is why I urge my children to hoard their possessions now.

For family holidays we used to hire a car – we didn't own a vehicle until I was about ten years old – and my father drove us up to the popular beach resort of Mar del Plata, which was about six hours from home. Six hours at least, in those days. I have great memories of those trips to the seaside, even though I couldn't swim.

Some of my most entertaining days as a child were provided by local dances that were held in various corners of our remote region. The venue would be a little bar somewhere, just a simple room with a small serving area and an open dance floor big enough to accommodate a large assembly of local farmers and their families. The music was provided by a live band, complete with drummer, guitarist, accordion player and singer. It was a typical *gaucho* affair.

These events used to generate a small amount of cash, but more importantly they were great social gatherings. There were huge distances separating the houses where we lived, so these days offered a welcome opportunity to mix with the locals, some of whom, by the way, were excellent dancers. I stood and watched in awe at what seemed like professional performers to a wide-eyed youth such as myself. The tango, the paso doble, the waltz – they mastered them all. There were some seriously impressive dancers who starred at these events. It's safe to say that I wasn't one of them, however. Not that it stopped me from trying!

From the age of about 11 or 12 years old I used to attend the dances, along with a whole host of other people from *el campo*. My mother made me wear shorts so that I could show off my nice legs! I was inspired by the choreographed manner in which the locals danced. They were so slick, so cool. I wanted to dance like them. I loved the rhythm of the music and used to throw myself onto the dance floor. Unfortunately I had no rhythm myself. Energy yes, bundles of it in fact, but rhythm definitely not. I would leap onto the floor in my shorts and frantically contort myself into a variety of positions that, as far as I was concerned, were perfectly matched to the music. Before long, though, someone nearby would decide that enough was enough, and I'd be dragged off mid-performance. "Look at Ricky," I'd hear them say. "He's such a bad dancer." Even though my dancing ability failed to match my enthusiasm I never got tired of trying. I quite happily took centre stage, even if I was hopelessly uncoordinated. I would also stand up and recite poetry at local festivals. I was uninhibited as a kid, quite expressive really. That side of my character was perhaps evident in the way that I played football throughout my career. I wanted to impress. I craved the audience's applause.

As a child, an event that I looked forward to with even more relish than the local dances was a traditional once-a-year gathering at our house that wasn't Christmas or a birthday celebration. It was the annual castration of the bulls. That may not sound like the most glamorous of events; it probably doesn't sound like much fun at all. My wife Cristina, for one, gets bored senseless at the mere mention of such occasions. "Not again," she says, especially if we're about to eat. I can appreciate that. I'm sure there are more appropriate subjects to discuss around the dinner table. But it is part of my culture. And as an impressionable young boy I found it all quite fascinating.

The bulls weren't castrated just for the hell of it. It was necessary to control the cattle population. My father would invite 20 or 30 people to our house for the ritual. I used to watch these big *gauchos* arrive on their big horses carrying big swords, some with intricately carved bone handles and each carried like a badge of honour. They would lasso a bull, put their weight on it to hold the animal down and castrate it with one clean swipe of their blade. I was so impressed by these powerful men. They had a real aura, and – to me – were shrouded in mystery. They rode in from nowhere, carrying sabres in their belts so long they had to walk through doors sideways (or so the farmers used to joke). They did their business, wrestling the bulls to the ground and cutting their balls off. Then they would sit around the fire, telling stories of past escapades, before riding off into the night. I didn't have television or the movies from which to derive my early childhood idols. My heroes were right there in Roque Pérez.

While the adults sat by the fire eating the products of their day's work – that may not sound at all appetising to some, I know, but bulls' testicles are a delicacy in Argentina – I occasionally sloped off to see the castrated animals. Not to check on their welfare, but to ride them like a cowboy. I was seven or eight years old, and the only chance I had of staying on these beasts like a rodeo man was by jumping on when castration had rendered them virtually lifeless. My plan never quite worked though. They still threw me off like a rag doll. This kind of routine is completely foreign to many people. I'm aware of that of course. But it was embedded in my culture. I grew up in that environment and that was how we lived. That's how several generations of my family lived. I'm proud of my heritage. I was a *gaucho* first and a footballer second.

Other occasions I remember include the *velatorio* that followed the passing of my grandmother Rosa. A *velatorio* is like a wake, where the body of the deceased is placed on show at the house of their family. People come from far and wide to pay their respects and to say a final farewell. Nobody came by car in those days, but a massive stream of people rode in on their horses for my grandmother's *velatorio*. They travelled a long way, and we provided food for all of them. Certain aspects of that day are quite amusing when I look back now. I recall thinking, "I didn't realise my grandmother knew so many people." The fact that I didn't even recognise some of them made me wonder if a few of our visitors were not friends or family at all, just hungry locals in search of a free lunch.

Reminiscing about my upbringing is something I can do with great fondness. I was a happy child, surrounded by a loving family. But despite looking back with a strong sense of nostalgia I can't pretend there weren't hard times too. There was one emotion in particular I remember feeling as a child that wasn't so positive, an underlying concern that was a constant source of torment. I felt a deep-rooted sense of injustice.

My father rented a plot of land and the whole family worked hard around the farm so that we could pay the rent. It was a tough existence. We were always on the breadline, and there was never a surplus of cash. I'll never forget the visits we used to get from the accountant who represented the landowners. He would turn up in his suit to claim the rent, or to impose a new tariff. He was so clinical, so cold. He had no understanding of our plight. He didn't care if our crop yield was low because it hadn't rained; he was only interested in collecting his money. My father was a decent, hard-working man. He was given no leeway at all though.

That suited figure didn't know what it was like to struggle, to work so hard just to make ends meet. Or how difficult it was when you were able to use your car just once a week because you couldn't afford any more fuel. I can clearly remember as a child how we felt the economic situation as a family, and it left me with a bitter, unjust feeling that has remained ever since. Farmers were under so much pressure. Some years were good, don't get me wrong, but others were bad. To a large extent our futures were in the lap of the gods. When we sowed our seeds, we knew our livelihood depended on the weather and other factors. The wait was tortuous. A baby calf would be born and we had to pray that it didn't become ill or infected in the next six months, which would scupper our chances of selling it.

I honestly believe that, even if I hadn't been a footballer, I wouldn't have been a *peón*. I would have found something else – maybe farm-related – but not a job where I was dedicating my life simply to paying the rent. I would have fought tooth and nail to avoid that. I knew what it was like to get up at dawn and work. I was happy as a child, I genuinely was, but I never had money. My parents weren't able to hand me ten pesos and say, "Go and get yourself something." I was always dealing with limits.

In the midst of all that, however, I was convinced that I knew of a way out. From that lonely, isolated place, I had this strong conviction – from the age of maybe ten or 11 years old – that I would be a footballer. At precisely what level, I didn't know. What I was aware of, though, was the need to spend every spare second with that ball at my feet. I practised until my sandals wore out. "Don't worry, Mama," I would say. "One day I'll be able to pay for brand new ones. One day I'll be famous." I was sure that football would offer an escape route. And it did. Football allowed me to live a dignified live, to travel the world, to have a beautiful family and to educate my children. That ball – *la pelota* – saved me.

Chapter Two
HEROES

José Sanfilippo may not be a familiar name in England, and – beyond the boundaries of South America at least – he is unlikely to feature in many discussions regarding the game's most outstanding football players of the last century. But the mere mention of the former San Lorenzo striker still evokes the fondest of memories for me. José Sanfilippo was my idol.

My earliest recollections of organised football are dominated by the booming sound of those four syllables *"SAN-FI-LI-PPO"*, with the announcement of his name usually accompanied by a protracted cry of *"GOOOOOOOOL"* from an excited radio broadcaster. That, in turn, would trigger another noisy outpouring of joy in a distant corner of the province – the Villa household. Every weekend I would sit by the radio with my father and listen intently to every word of the football reports. Speaking in our house during this time was strictly forbidden. Silence was demanded. Even the animals had to keep quiet.

There was only one team for us – Club Atlético San Lorenzo de Almagro, or just San Lorenzo to use their more familiar title. One of Buenos Aires's *cinco grandes* ('Big Five'), along with Boca Juniors, River Plate, Independiente and Racing Club, San Lorenzo remains the club I support to this day (along with Tottenham, of course, albeit from a much further distance). My son, too, is a fan. The history of San Lorenzo is punctuated by a couple of outstanding achievements, for which the players responsible each time will for ever be fêted. Champions of Argentina in 1946, San Lorenzo toured Europe the year after, where they gave a stunning account of themselves by beating the national teams of both Spain and Portugal. Two decades later, the club cruised to the *Metropolitano* title in 1968 without losing a single game (the league season in Argentina used to be split into two – the Metropolitano, contested by teams from the major cities, and then the *Nacional*, contested by teams from all regions). Such was their domination, the class of '68 became known as *Los Matadores* ('the Killers'). My dream was to run out at *el Estadio Gasómetro* in the *azulgrana* (blue and red) of San Lorenzo, and to one day occupy my own place in the club's history.

Choosing a favourite player to adopt as one's hero was hardly a difficult decision for an impressionable young follower of *el Azulgrana*, not when you had José Francisco Sanfilippo in your team. For four consecutive seasons – in 1958, 1959, 1960 and 1961 – Sanfilippo topped the goalscoring charts in Argentina. International recognition duly followed, and the star of Argentina's domestic game represented the national team with similar distinction. His 21 goals for Argentina, in just 29 appearances, included one against England at the 1962 World Cup in Chile; unfortunately for Argentina, Bobby Charlton and Jimmy Greaves were also on target that day, and England won the match 3-1.

Nicknamed *el Nene* ('the Kid') after emerging from the youth ranks at San Lorenzo, the prolific Sanfilippo had short black hair and a muscular frame. Not that I had much idea of what he looked like back then. We didn't have a television, so the only images I had were those conjured up in my mind in response to the commentator's detailed description of events. When I was a kid all I could ever think about was becoming a professional footballer, and my thoughts would often drift towards Sanfilippo. Exactly how did he live his life? What sort of food did he eat? Did he sleep in a massive bed? Just what was it that made him so special? This is typical, I suppose, of any young star-struck supporter. As I grew older and eventually achieved my dream of playing at the top level, I realised that footballers are essentially the same as everyone else, and not the superhuman creatures that you imagine as a child. I never forgot about those youthful misconceptions, though, and made every effort to satisfy each request for an autograph from young supporters, and still do to this day, because I can remember what it felt like to crave such a memento.

While José Sanfilippo can claim to have played a significant role in shaping my boyhood ambitions, he was an almost mythical character as far as I was concerned. I listened patiently for any mention of his name on the radio, but seeing him perform in the flesh was a distant dream – I didn't attend a professional match until I was 17 – and so too, for a long time, was watching him on TV.

What I needed was a real life hero, and before long I stumbled across one. Not in the lofty surroundings of the country's leading division, but way down the footballing ladder; never mind Boca Juniors or River Plate, Independiente or my beloved San Lorenzo, I found the most incredible player to marvel at right under my nose.

Football is everywhere in Argentina, and Roque Pérez is no exception. The town, just like numerous others up and down the nation, is intensely passionate about the game. Any organised matches draw an admiring crowd, whether it be a fiercely-contested six-a-side tournament on the dirt pitch of *La Chingada* or an even more fiercely contested 11-a-side fixture between neighbouring towns. When local pride is at stake the people come out in force, and absolutely no quarter is given.

I loved the excitement and intensity of those local league games, and I would eagerly join around 2,000 other spectators on a regular basis to witness such events. The team I wanted to watch more than any other during my early teenage years came from Las Tunas, a town situated some ten kilometres from Roque Pérez. And it was all because of one player. His name was Jorge *el Negro* Nievas. I was in awe of his style, and was almost as mesmerised by his dazzling skills as the defenders he constantly left trailing in his wake. *El Negro* (known as such because of his black hair) had so many ways of beating an opponent. If he wasn't rolling the ball through their legs (*un caño*, as we say in Argentina) or flicking it over their heads, he'd be navigating his way to goal via a series of swerves and dummies.

I had a sure sense right there and then that this was the kind of player I wanted to emulate. Sanfilippo was a prolific goalscorer, one of the finest that Argentina has ever produced. But – and this may sound unusual – the glory of football for me wasn't in scoring the goals. I was happy to let someone else assume the Sanfilippo role. From a young age I just wanted to entertain, to take players on. My objective was to perform in a manner that would excite the crowd. That was my dream. I wanted to play like Nievas.

The fact that a professional career eluded Nievas can be explained by his slack approach to the game. He was at Vélez Sarsfield, another of the many Buenos Aires-based clubs, but a reluctance to commit wholly to the life of a full-time footballer meant that he failed to establish himself at the highest level. He was content to play alongside his friends at a lower, albeit good-quality, level. He worked at a Mercedes-Benz factory in González Catán on the outskirts of Buenos Aires, with his income supplemented by an assortment of local amateur teams. A permanent commitment to football wasn't for him. In other words, he wasn't the keenest of trainers. My own aspirations of imitating the ways of Nievas appear to have included his idle approach to training; any number of my former teammates, I'm afraid to say, will no doubt testify to this. I met Nievas some years later, after I'd turned professional, and told him that he was the player I tried to copy. It was great to meet him, even if he did seem a little surprised. Sanfilippo, on the other hand, is now an outspoken media pundit. I must admit I'm not such a fan of his now.

Santiago Larre was the first club I ever played for. They may have been a modest provincial outfit, but I could barely have felt more excited had it been Real Madrid or Barcelona. I was 12 years old and part of a team. All those hours of solitary practice, all that time spent perfecting my control alone in the dusty surroundings of my home, could now be applied to real game situations. Joining Santiago Larre seemed like a natural move for me to make. My Uncle Mario, who was a decent player, represented their first-team and my father had also played for them. In addition to that a few of my cousins were affiliated to the club; with such a strong family connection it was inevitable really that I would one day follow suit.

Sundays could never come around quick enough for me. That was when a group of us from Roque Pérez would bundle into the car – a vehicle that my grandmother bought for the family – and set off for Larre, with my father behind the wheel. The 25 kilometre trek was too far to travel on horseback. That creaky old car had seen better days, and the roads were hardly the most sophisticated, so our journey usually lasted around an hour. Give or take a few minutes, that is, to allow for the odd puncture that often disrupted our bumpy ride.

Three games were held each Sunday, with the youth team kicking-off first, at around 11 o'clock in the morning, followed by the reserves and then the first-team later that afternoon. To begin with, I would play in the first game and then stay to watch the seniors perform. Not just because I wanted to see the club's leading men in action, but because I was desperate to get some more time out on the pitch myself. I sat patiently on the sidelines, before racing towards one of the goals with my friends for shooting practice each time the referee's whistle signalled a half-time break or the end of a match.

Those days were brilliant. It was a real social occasion every time, a chance to meet up with family and friends. Larre itself was nothing more than a small village, or hamlet. It consisted of a school, a shop and a train stop used primarily by farmers to transport their grain and cattle. And there was a football pitch of course. On Sundays, the place came alive. By the time the first-team match was about to start – the main event – a crowd of around 500-600 would regularly gather, all standing around the perimeter of the pitch. Sometimes, for a really big game, that figure would reach 1,000. The people came from surrounding farms, with almost everyone riding to the ground on their horses.

The feeling of slipping on a Santiago Larre shirt for the first time was exhilarating. It was a moment to cherish, and with the team's colours matching those of San Lorenzo – blue and red stripes – my sense of pride was enhanced further still. Even though I was only 12 I began my 'club' career in the under-15 side. On reflection, the experience of playing against boys a couple of years older than me was invaluable. Being confronted with opponents who were bigger and stronger significantly accelerated my development, because I had to find alternative means by which to succeed in one-on-one situations. I had to be intelligent. I had to be tricky. I soon learned that craft and guile were essential attributes, and became a more skilful player as a result.

By the age of 14 I was playing alongside the men, before my notable progression was rewarded with a first-team debut at 15. I also appeared for the Roque Pérez representative team, and my form did not go unnoticed beyond the confines of my local region. The first party to declare an interest was Club Atlético Huracán, the Buenos Aires-based club from which Tottenham Hotspur would later sign a certain Osvaldo Ardiles. They offered me a trial, and at 16 years of age I was presented with a golden opportunity to make a name for myself.

It was a chance I'd been longing for, and I was determined to make the most of it. I felt I performed well in the trial and, sure enough, so too did my potential employers. Huracán wanted to sign me – "Wonderful," I thought. They didn't, however, want to pay me – "Not so wonderful," I thought. Playing football was still my dream, and I was willing to make the necessary sacrifices to realise it. But living in the city without a regular wage was just not feasible. I expressed my gratitude, but said "No thanks." I would have to wait a little longer for my big break.

Not too long though. Quilmes Atlético Club, yet another club from the capital, were next to take notice. Quilmes is one of Argentina's oldest surviving clubs, having been founded as Quilmes Rovers at the back end of the 19th century by a British man who was teaching in the city. It is also the club from which I launched my professional career, and because of that I will always regard *el Cervecero* ('the Brewers' – because the famous Quilmes beer is brewed there) with great affection.

Quilmes were keen to take a closer look at the best Roque Pérez had to offer, and invited me and four other players from the town for a trial. The fact that two of the other four lads were cousins of mine – Mario Villa and Manuel Ormazabal – definitely helped the three of us feel at ease, and without doubt gave us an advantage in the practice match that would decide our fate. Again the trial went well, and again the representatives of my prospective new club were interested. This time, however, there was a financial offering. Not a particularly large financial offering, it has to be said – I was paid next to nothing – but enough to tempt me to the city. My occupation was now officially that of a *futbolista*.

That was just as well, because the alternatives at the time weren't exactly filling me with excitement. My career options were fairly limited I would say. I don't really know what I would have done had I not been a footballer. One thing's for sure – I would never have worked in an office. No thanks! I couldn't have spent my days sat behind a desk, not when you consider the expansive environment in which I was brought up. No way. Whatever my profession was going to be it would have to be based outside. I knew that much. I get headaches if I can't see a long stretch of open land in front of me. I need to see the horizon.

I did have one paid job before football came calling. I drove a tractor on one of the farms close to my home. From midday until eight o'clock at night I sat on that machine planting crops. Eight hours a day, seven days a week. It was so noisy. I'll never forget the tranquillity that came with turning the engine off at the end of a shift: complete silence. For six months I ploughed that land, before the offer from Quilmes meant that I could park up the tractor for good and save my eardrums from a further pounding.

There was one other job I was destined to do but somehow managed to avoid – national service. The national service draw was a huge event, announced live on the radio. It was incredibly tense because the one-year military term wasn't compulsory for every 18-year-old, just those named in the draw. The system involved everyone having an ID card complete with a personal number, with a certain range of numbers excluded from the draft.

I had not long been at Quilmes when the time of my potential call-up came around. It was a particular concern for a footballer, because losing a year of your career at that age can have serious consequences. Some people, not just football players, went to great lengths to avoid carrying out national service. It wasn't unheard of for lawyers to be paid considerable sums of money to invent a reason why their client could not possibly accept the call-up. I listened to the draw on the radio along with all of my family. The last three digits of each ID number were the vital figures. It was announced that all numbers from 001 to 156 were exempt. My last three digits were 012. I missed the cut!

I celebrated like I'd won the lottery. I didn't have much money so I was hardly in a position to throw an extravagant party. Instead I bought a cheap bottle of sparkling wine and a cake to share between six of us. That roughly amounted to a couple of sips of wine and a slither of cake each but I didn't care. I was so relieved.

Quilmes covered the cost of my accommodation and food, and for a teenage boy accustomed to life in the country it was an enlightening time for me. My new home housed six or seven players in all, and over the ensuing months the experience instilled a sense of discipline – there were certain curfews we had to abide by – and responsibility in each one of us. I was forced to grow up fast.

It was at this time that I met Anibal Diaz, a man who had a major influence on my development during the formative stage of my career. Diaz was a director of football at Quilmes and was constantly offering advice. He was a perceptive man, a good reader of people. He had that knack of knowing how to deal with individual players, with his treatment tailored to suit the specific personality of each one. After each game, for example, he would say to me: "Go home, Ricky; we'll see you on Monday." He knew how close I was to my family, and how attached I was to my home town. He was also aware of the many distractions that a big city such as Buenos Aires offers, and of the potentially damaging effect such temptations could have on a young man attempting to establish himself as a professional sportsman. I have a great deal to thank him for.

So after every match I would make a quick dash to catch

the last train back to Roque Pérez. I was usually armed with a sandwich and a Coca-Cola, which was just about all I could afford to purchase back then. But I can't say that a lack of money really bothered me, and neither did the three hours it took for the train to amble between Buenos Aires and Roque Pérez. Even if we'd lost the match, once I was on that train and home was on the horizon I was happy.

While the senior side at Quilmes were competing alongside Argentina's finest I was content to start out with my contemporaries in the under-17s. I felt comfortable in my new surroundings, and seemed to acquit myself reasonably well. Then, just six months after first appearing for the youth team, I was catapulted into the spotlight.

Player unrest in Argentina is hardly a rare phenomenon, and I have one such occurrence to thank for handing me my top-flight debut. It was September 1970, and the Quilmes camp was not a happy one. The senior players had not been paid, which was not exactly unheard of in Argentina, and decided that the threat of strike action was their only option. The president responded by suspending the entire squad and, all of a sudden, Quilmes had a problem. How could they fulfil their scheduled fixtures without any players? The club had no alternative but to delve into the reserve and youth ranks, and the selection of players they came up with to replace the temporary absentees included an 18-year-old Ricardo Villa. I was about to be given an unexpected introduction to first-team football.

Our opponents were Huracán and, for a reason I can't quite remember, the setting was not Huracán's home ground but Boca Juniors' famous *Bombonera* stadium. When Boca play at home their fanatical supporters sing incessantly, bouncing up and down as one on the terraces behind each goal. The sustained movement creates such a force that the vibrations can be felt throughout the rest of the stadium. It really is a sight to behold. This, though, wasn't one of those occasions. News had circulated that Quilmes would be fielding an under-strength team and, as a consequence, a crowd that can best be described as meagre gathered in small pockets around the ground. It was not quite as glamorous as I'd imagined top-rank football to be, but I was willing to accept my chance nonetheless. I wanted to test myself against the very best, to learn about life at the highest level.

We were certainly taught a lesson in *la Bombonera* that day. For those of you expecting a fairytale victory for the rank outsiders, a heroic triumph for the gallant underdog, it may be best to look away now. We lost 5-0. And it could have been much worse. It was men against boys in every sense. Even when we did get possession of the ball, our opponents showed little urgency in trying to retrieve it. They were convinced it would soon find its way back to them, and more often than not they were right.

But, while the team took a comprehensive beating, I actu-ally quite enjoyed the occasion. Playing on the left side of midfield, my initial assessment at the end of the game was that I'd given a fair account of myself. That positive self-analysis was endorsed by complimentary reports regarding my performance in the following day's newspapers. Even more uplifting than that, however, were the post-match words of a celebrated opponent. The sound of the final whistle prompted the customary round of backslaps and handshakes, as the victors – who'd barely broken a sweat – exchanged pleasant-ries with their awestruck victims. One of the Huracán players made his way towards me, offering not only a handshake but also a message of encouragement. I recognised the familiar figure straight away. It was Héctor *el Bambino* Veira.

"Well done," he said. "You're a good player. Keep on like that and you'll be fine."

I was stunned. Talk about a shot of confidence. *El Bambino* was a San Lorenzo legend. He was at the heart of *los Matadores*, the unbeaten championship-winning side of 1968. He was one of my heroes. His was one of the names that used to pepper the radio reports I listened to religiously as a child, when every San Lorenzo goal had me leaping with joy. If José Sanfilippo hadn't scored it then Veira usually had. Sharing a pitch with the man was hard enough to comprehend. Now he was going out of his way to talk to me. To praise my performance! I've never left the field after a 5-0 thrashing feeling so good.

Another defeat followed in our next game, by a single goal against Los Andes, which prompted the president to lift the suspension imposed on the first-team regulars. For many of the stand-in squad that meant a return to action in the lower reaches, but not for me. I retained my place in the senior side, and managed to stay there for a number of years.

Despite reinforcing the team with a returning crop of first-choice players, Quilmes was still an unsettled club as that 1970 campaign drew to a close. After finishing 15th out of 21 teams in the regular season we embarked on a series of play-off matches that gave us more than one chance to secure our elite status for another year at least. Unfortunately we managed to spurn each and every one of those opportunities, so our fate eventually hinged on our final match of the season, against Ferro Carril Oeste. While we limped towards the finishing line that year our opponents swept into the game on a wave of positive momentum. Buenos Aires-based Ferro Carril Oeste may have been a second division side, but they were very much in the ascendancy after emerging triumphant from a play-off group staged to determine which two teams from the second tier would be handed a chance to swap places with the two teetering top-flight outfits that were my team, Quilmes, and Colon.

Everyone played each other once in the four-team group, with our future resting on the outcome of our last match. Without doubt it was the biggest game of my life up to that point. The stakes were high, and so too was the attendance inside the neutral venue of *Estadio Tomás Adolfo Ducó*, the home ground of Club Atlético Huracán. I was named as a substitute for a game in which we needed just a draw to retain our top-flight status.

In matches of such magnitude it's so important to start well, to begin at a good tempo, to stay fully concentrated and, crucially, to score the first goal. After just a few minutes we were 1-0 down. So much for making that bright start. Then, with little more than a quarter of an hour gone, it became evident that one of our midfielders was carrying an injury. The manager, *Chupete* Alegre, cast his eye over the bench. Looking back at him, as his side trailed 1-0 to a team clearly motivated for this critical encounter, was a huddle of men not exactly straining at the leash to get on the pitch. Even back then in Argentina teams were allowed to name five substitutes. But with the pressure on and the side trailing, there was hardly a scramble amongst the reserves to join the action.

Then the Quilmes supporters started to chant "VILLA!

VILLA!" "Can't they sing someone else's name?" I thought. Perhaps swayed by the fans' outburst, the manager gave me the nod to warm up. And then I was on. With 17 minutes played, my team a goal down and my name ringing out around the ground, the stage was set. What a perfect time to announce myself at the top table. Only I didn't. I'd love to say I scored two, or even three goals to keep us up, but I barely touched the ball and we lost 4-0. Again, no fairytale finish.

This was the stark reality of professional football. It was a disastrous result for Quilmes and, as they tend to do in Argentina, our supporters made sure we knew it. Full of fury and aggression, those fans in Quilmes colours made their way towards the front of the stands, from where their venomous volleys could be delivered with maximum impact. Their mode of attack wasn't just verbal either – they were not averse to throwing the odd object or two – and some players did, inevitably perhaps, respond. "After I've showered I'll see you outside," suggested at least one of our players.

All in all, the whole situation left me feeling pretty dejected. The team had been relegated, the players were unhappy, the supporters were angry and I had no money. Things couldn't have been much worse. Or so I thought. In actual fact, things *were* about to get worse. I was about to experience the brutal 'delights' of Argentina's second division.

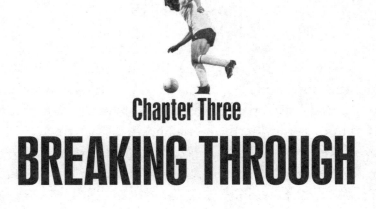

Chapter Three

BREAKING THROUGH

The thing I remember most about Mastro Mauro is his sideburns. Long, thick, dark sideburns, masking the chiselled jawline of a hardened face. Mastro Mauro was tough, a big, barrel-chested central midfielder accustomed to the cruder side of Argentine football. What I also remember about Mastro Mauro is that he once threatened to kill me.

I'm pretty sure he didn't mean it, but at the time I wasn't prepared to take any chances. He'd already issued one warning in the midst of a game against his team, Nueva Chicago – something along the lines of "If you go past me I will smash you" – before he decided to turn up the heat. "See them over there?" he said, standing beside me in the centre of the pitch and pointing towards a savage-looking pack of Nueva Chicago supporters. "Between me and that lot we're going to kill you in a minute." I didn't panic on hearing Mastro's threat to encourage a little crowd participation that day, and I wouldn't say I was intimidated. But I definitely kept an eye out for the big man. I respected him. And I certainly didn't try to nutmeg him. This was second division football, and I had to get used to it.

Relegation for Quilmes in 1970 sparked a mass exodus of

senior players. With only a handful of games behind me I had little option but to stay, and the club was once again forced to rely heavily on a smattering of youth team products as Quilmes began life in the second tier. That three of those players went on to become World Cup winners in 1978 – myself, Daniel Bertoni and Ubaldo *Pato* Fillol – proves the club were at least doing something right. Both Bertoni and Fillol enjoyed notable careers in the game having served their apprenticeship, as I did, with *el Cervecero*. Bertoni scored the goal that clinched victory in the World Cup final, after which he scored plenty more goals during successful club stints in Spain and Italy. Fillol was, in my opinion, quite simply the best goalkeeper Argentina has ever produced. Nicknamed *el Pato* ('the Duck'), he was one of the players with whom I shared a house whilst employed by Quilmes.

Stopping the slide after dropping down a division proved extremely difficult for our young team. In truth, we were closer to fighting relegation (again) than fighting for the title. As for the general experience of operating at that level – the standard of playing surfaces, the style of football and, especially, the primitive behaviour of the supporters – it was like nothing else I'd ever known.

One of several differences I noticed between playing football in Argentina and England is the conduct of the supporters. I'm aware that in England there is a history of hooliganism, with violent clashes at home and abroad staining the English game for a number of years in the 1970s and 1980s. But the difference in Argentina is that the fans do not just fight each other; they are aggressive towards the players, sometimes physically. Although some grounds in England were a little hostile – I remember Middlesbrough fans being particularly unfriendly – I found English supporters to be most respectful of the players, polite even.

Getting off the team coach for an away match was not a harrowing experience in England, whereas in Argentina it was always an ordeal. Especially when you visited smaller clubs in the backwaters of the city or its provinces. Locals would greet your arrival with a kick and a slap. The police looked the other way, although if we were lucky they would come – at a leisurely stroll – to our assistance. Usually after a few blows had been landed. Changing rooms just about offered some sort of refuge, so that was where we would often sit for lengthy periods after games as we waited for the baying crowds at the door to disperse.

Only when we were out on the playing field did we feel protected. That was because all those in attendance were penned back behind 15-foot-high metal fences that ran along the entire perimeter of the pitch. Curving inwards at the top and trimmed with a barbed-wire edge, these barriers acted as an effective deterrent to those intent on getting up close and personal with the players. Not that it stopped some from trying, and when an opening did arise in the fence the savages would race onto the pitch like a pack of wild dogs.

It was like playing in a prison.

While the fencing kept spectators at bay in a physical sense, it was impossible to control other aspects of their conduct. Such was their close proximity to the playing area that venturing towards the edge of the pitch was never a pleasant experience; the designated corner-taker often bore the brunt of it, as he placed himself within spitting distance of the crowd as he prepared to take each kick. They didn't always spit at the players; sometimes they threw plastic bottles filled with urine.

Verbal abuse was commonplace. "Villa you lazy bastard" they would shout. And that was just our fans. I would sometimes respond and become embroiled in a spiky exchange of words, and then make sure I was looking over my shoulder when I left the ground after the match. I never reacted well to that sort of castigation. It certainly didn't spur me on. On the contrary, it served only to drain my motivation.

Despite all those difficulties I must have been showing some signs of promise. In 1971 I was included in the Argentina under-18 squad that travelled to Cannes for an eight-team tournament. I spent most of the competition on the bench, but we finished third and I was mixing with some outstanding young players who were already playing in the Argentine top-flight. It was an early taste of international football and I wanted more of it. I played on foreign soil again the following year, this time for a second division representative team that visited Israel, Yugoslavia and Greece on a badly-organised trip that involved (a) lots of incredibly long coach journeys and (b) a few scheduled games being scrapped because the opposition failed to show up.

Playing outside the top-flight for Quilmes was not the most fun I've ever had. The pitches were worn and patchy, and most teams opted for brute strength over style. Every game was like a war. Even when we won I wasn't completely happy. I was disillusioned. I needed a break, and in 1973 I got one. Club Atlético San Martín, based in the north-western province of Tucumán, were playing in the Nacional championship at the time and identified me as a player who could help them consolidate their status as a top-flight club. I jumped at the chance of joining them on a short-term loan deal. After three years away from the top tier I now had an opportunity to show I was worthy of taking my place back in it. My first game was against Newell's Old Boys of Rosario. Losing 5-2 was a deflating experience for the team, but on a personal level I could take some consolation. I came off the bench to score one of our goals, which may not have salvaged a positive result, but it did earn me a place in the starting line-up for the next match. And that's when things started to get interesting for me.

There's nothing quite like scoring a great goal against a great club to instantly raise a player's stock. Fortunately for me, several thousands of miles from Wembley and several years before I'd even heard of a team called Tottenham Hotspur, I managed to do it. River Plate were the opponents, and to appreciate the club's standing in Argentina just think Manchester United in England, Barcelona or Real Madrid in Spain, Bayern Munich in Germany or Juventus, Inter or AC Milan in Italy. Alongside Boca Juniors, River – or *los Millonarios* ('the Millionaires') as they've been commonly referred to since acquiring a reputation as big spenders many years ago – is the country's most celebrated club. Name an Argentinian player of significant renown and the chances are he represented one of these two colossal institutions, whether it be Rattín, Maradona, Tévez or Riquelme (all Boca) or Sívori, Di Stefano, Passarella, Kempes or Crespo (River Plate). Some, such as Batistuta and Caniggia, played for both.

The visit of River Plate in October 1973 drew a crowd of around 30,000 to Tucumán, with a distance of almost 700 miles from the capital restricting the number of travelling fans. The majority of those in attendance, therefore, were supporting the home team. So silence fell across much of the ground when River went ahead, even if it wasn't a great surprise. Our visitors had won their first two games that season, while our previous match had ended in a 5-2 defeat. We were very much the underdogs. Then, out of nothing, it happened. The ball dropped between me and a couple of River defenders deep inside our opponents' half. I was quickest to react, touching the ball away from the first defender and flicking it over his colleague. The home supporters roared their approval. Another defender was left behind as I advanced into the penalty area. The goalkeeper came flying out. I breezed past him. The rest was simple. It was all square and the place erupted. I had just conjured up the first defining moment of my career. We eventually lost the match 3-2, but all the talk afterwards revolved around my goal. "This boy Ricky Villa belongs in the top-flight" I heard people say. Before the game, they didn't even know my name.

My exploits against River Plate didn't quite change things overnight. San Martín did not have an option to buy me at that stage, so on completion of my loan spell in early-1974 I returned to Quilmes. I was confident, however, that I wouldn't be there for long. I had performed well enough in my brief time up north to prompt murmurs within the game suggesting I was a player of real potential. I was certainly ready to move on. In the six months that passed as I – and cash-strapped Quilmes – waited for a decent offer I was living in the same house as when I first joined them, was still getting paid a pittance and still couldn't afford to buy a car. In fact, the 'riches' I had amassed in four and a half years as a Quilmes employee allowed me to purchase a small television set and a car radio for my father. And little else.

When an offer did eventually materialise it looked, at first, as though my desired switch would be scuppered. The identity of the club making a move for me was, not unexpectedly perhaps, San Martín. Having already spent time there it seemed a logical move to make, although Quilmes's demand for a transfer fee of 33 million pesos (the equivalent at the time, I would guess, of around £250,000) proved to be something of an obstacle. "We'll get back to you," responded San Martín officials. They had a plan. It was a simple plan aimed at raising the necessary funds to complete the deal: they had a big whip-round. It was a flattering gesture and, after exploring various avenues, the club and its supporters managed to stump up a total of 30 million pesos. Final offer. A stubborn Quilmes president, showing not the slightest hint of compassion, refused to budge.

I was destined for a move to Tucumán, only not to join San Martín. As negotiations remained in a state of deadlock, San Martín's fierce rivals Atlético Tucumán entered proceedings by slapping the required 33 million on the table – whilst no doubt aiming a smug glance in the direction of their neighbouring club – and that was that. I was now Ricardo Villa of Atlético Tucumán.

Having served my time on the murkier side of the fence I was a top-flight player again. It was an important step up for me, and that progression was reflected in the financial terms I accepted at my new club. It's easy to say, I know, but money has really never been the major motivating force in my life. Having said that, I certainly welcomed my newly-acquired wealthy status – who wouldn't? – and with the six and a half million pesos I received as a signing-on fee I immediately bought my first apartment.

Regardless of the financial benefits, the move was fantastic for me. Far from the frenetic, scrambled approach I'd begrudgingly become accustomed to at Quilmes, Atlético were a technically sound side with players who liked the ball at their feet and believed that passing their way to goal was the most effective mode of attack. I'd finally found a team to which I felt completely suited. My game was all about picking the ball up and dictating attacks, running at defenders and creating openings, and at Atlético I was afforded the perfect platform to do just that. It was a team moulded in my style. A match made in heaven, if you like.

Everything just clicked. I was in the form of my life, and the Atlético Tucumán supporters were quick to show their appreciation. I believe an idol is a player who is almost above criticism from the fans, someone who is forgiven the odd poor performance because they are trusted to deliver in the long term. This is the status I enjoyed at Atlético. Such was my form that in 1976 I was granted a new contract. Finally, I was in a position to do something I'd long dreamed of. I went out and purchased my first car.

To most professional footballers of the modern era, thumbing a lift home from football on a Saturday night is, I would guess, a completely alien concept. Then again, so too is growing up on a farm and milking cows every morning. But that was the life I knew. During my early years as a full-time player I would catch the train back from Buenos Aires to Roque Pérez after a match and complete the final 15 kilometres of my journey home by flagging down a passing vehicle heading along the dusty road that led towards *el campo*. By establishing myself in Tucumán I could consign those convoluted travel plans to the past.

Buying my first car represented a real milestone for me. It was a Peugeot 504, and of the three models on offer I opted for the cheapest one (I didn't want to get carried away!). When

I arrived at the garage I couldn't wait to finalise the deal. I kept getting handed various papers to sign and all I wanted to do was drive away in my new car. I remember sitting there with my legs shaking, I was so excited. Eventually I did get behind the wheel. I was the proud owner of my very own vehicle. My parents – my whole family in fact – and friends all congratulated me. It was something of a symbolic moment I suppose.

So I was flying off the pitch (we tend to drive a little recklessly in Argentina) and, I have to say, doing likewise on it. I was developing a knack of producing at just the right time – a habit that would serve me well later in my career, of course – and in a televised meeting with Gimnasia y Esgrima La Plata I once again demonstrated that uncanny sense of timing.

Friday night was football night in Argentina. It wasn't the day on which all the games were played, just the one selected match from each round of fixtures deemed sufficiently enticing to be broadcast live on television. With a watching audience of around two or three million it offered a rare opportunity for players to impose themselves on the football-following public; by scoring both goals in a 2-0 victory over Gimnasia that's exactly what I managed to do.

It was a breakthrough moment in a breakthrough year for me. Even the opposing supporters applauded my efforts, which is extremely rare in Argentina, and the following day's newspapers were equally generous in their praise. I felt like I was walking on the moon. Suddenly it seemed like the wait had been worthwhile. All those years spent dodging waist-high tackles and wayward missiles in the second division, all those uncomfortable visits to the most unwelcoming of venues.

Knowing that I'd embarked on that whole adventure just seemed to enhance my sense of achievement as I poured over the headlines. At 23 years of age I was sure, for the first time, that I had a real future in football.

With my confidence sky high I continued to play well as 1976 gave way to 1977. I was primarily a creative player, a number 10 who played 'free' behind the strikers. I was one of the players my colleagues, and the supporters, would look to for a spark of invention when opposing defences were proving frustratingly difficult to unlock. I couldn't always provide that invention – my form varied wildly from game to game throughout my career – but I was constantly probing for an opening. In addition to that, I scored a few goals, and never more prolifically than during my days at Atlético Tucumán. I registered 68 times in 108 appearances, which places me third on the club's list of all-time marksmen. It is a statistic of which I'm extremely proud, especially when you consider the fact that those occupying the first two places were both centre forwards. Atlético Tucumán fans even gave me the nickname 'God'! I'm sure that was based on a physical resemblance more than anything else though.

Scoring goals, of course, is a much sought-after quality, and I was aware of admiring glances from elsewhere. It was time to move on again, and time for me to claim a little piece of history.

Chapter Four
MILLION DOLLAR MAN

I n April 1979, almost one year after moving to England, I played for Tottenham against West Ham in a testimonial for Steve Perryman. Steve, who made his debut for the club as a 17-year-old in 1969, was outstanding as both a player and as a captain: the perfect professional. Ossie and I, however, were a little puzzled. Ten years at the same club . . . how on earth could that happen?

In Argentina, I should explain, this sort of extended stay with the same team is a notably rare occurrence. Virtually unthinkable. The only example that springs to mind is Ricardo Bochini, a marvellous player whom Diego Maradona cites as his idol. *El Bocha* spent his entire career with Independiente and, for that, remains the club's most prominent legend to this day. I love that, the enduring sense of association that comes with such loyalty. It allows one to assume a very honoured position, just as it has with Stevie and Bochini. On the whole, though, a different mentality exists in Argentina. Staying at one club for a number of years is generally regarded as lacking prestige in a way. Boring almost. So, by the January of 1977, another transfer had become inevitable. The move that followed, however, wasn't just another transfer. It was the most expensive exchange in the history of Argentine football.

The first club to express a genuine interest was Independiente. I had played for Tucumán in Tandil, which is in Buenos Aires Province, and after the game I was approached by a man called José Pastoriza. He was in charge of Independiente, and asked me if I would be interested in joining them. I said that of course I would! Pastoriza wasn't alone in chasing my signature, though. I was very much in demand at that time, even if I do say so myself. Other clubs made enquiries but in the end none of them could match the financial capacity of Racing Club. In an echo of my previous transfer, when I joined Atlético Tucumán after neighbours San Martín had failed to raise the necessary funds, I signed for Racing after fierce rivals Independiente had been priced out of the move. Racing president Horacio Rodriguez Larreta announced he was prepared to invest heavily in the team in order to appease his club's fanatical following and he wasn't bluffing. The exact figure varied across reports, with the exchange of goalkeeper Salomon also involved in the deal, but the fee was something like seven billion pesos. Due to Argentina's history of hyper-inflation it's hard to convert that figure into British pounds – about £500,000 maybe? – but either way it was crazy money. I remember a magazine publishing an article soon after, labelling me the 'Million Dollar Man' and listing all the extravagant purchases one could make with the same amount of money. "Look what you can buy with seven billion pesos instead of spending it on Ricky Villa" was the theme of the piece. A nice yacht, a big house in the country . . . the list went on.

Racing Club is one of the capital's top set of football clubs, the *cinco grandes* or 'Big Five'. Situated in Avellaneda, the industrial hub of Buenos Aires, Racing's home ground is the huge, bowl-like *Estadio Juan Domingo Perón*. Within shooting distance sits another impressive arena, the *Estadio Libertadores de América* where Racing's next-door neighbours and great rivals Independiente play. If British fans of a certain age are familiar with the name Racing it is probably because of a brutal World Club Championship clash with Celtic in 1967. Racing's reward for being crowned champions of South America earlier that year, following a narrow play-off victory over Nacional of Uruguay, was a meeting with Jock Stein's European Cup winners to decide who could rightfully claim to be the greatest club side on the planet. It was meant to be a prestigious showpiece event, but what followed was a shameful battle typical of many that blighted the intercontinental competition during the early years of its existence.

Celtic brought a 1-0 first leg lead to Buenos Aires, where they lost their goalkeeper before the game had begun – he was struck by a missile thrown from the crowd – and then lost the match 2-1. With the rules stating that a play-off would determine the winner if each side were victorious in one of the initial two legs (regardless, in those days, of the aggregate score or away goals) a third match in Montevideo was arranged to decide the outcome. That's when things turned really nasty. A violent contest was littered with a succession of horrendous challenges, with riot police entering the field of play to separate brawling players. Reports vary as to whether five or six were sent off, probably because one of Celtic's dismissed players is believed to have stayed on the pitch amidst all the carnage. Racing, by the way, won the game 1-0, not that the result seemed to matter that much.

Ten years had passed by the time I joined Racing. The man at the helm was Alfio *Coco* Basile. He was a decent manager with a simple approach who would later have two spells in charge of the national team; in the first of those spells he led Argentina at the 1994 World Cup, while the second ended with his resignation in 2008 and was followed by the appointment of Diego Maradona. Basile's decision to sign me meant that, all of a sudden, I had become the most talked-about player in the country. I was thrust into the spotlight and, psychologically, this presented me with a considerable challenge. I was no longer an emerging prospect on the outskirts. I was the costliest player in Argentine history, and with that came huge expectations. The occasional below-par performance that was shrugged off in Tucumán would not be tolerated in the demanding surrounds of my new Avellaneda home.

Thankfully, my attempts to justify the enormous price-tag began in ideal fashion. Just one goal was enough for us to beat Chacarita Juniors in the rain on my debut, and I scored it. Perfect. It certainly wasn't a trademark finish – far-post headers were never my forte. But, much to the delight of myself, my new employers and Racing's hardcore supporters – *la Guardia Imperial* ('the Imperial Guard') – I was off the mark, barely an hour into my Racing career. That night I went back to Roque Pérez. Along with my then-girlfriend Cristina, I walked into a local bar that was packed full of people, many of them familiar faces, and as we entered everyone turned around. They all started applauding. It was really quite a touching moment.

Unfortunately, that dream start was not a sign of things to come. The burden of that substantial fee proved a heavy weight to carry, and I constantly felt under pressure to produce my best form in every single game. That pressure was magnified by an understandably expectant group of supporters. Traditionally, the Racing fans like to see their team play with aggression, working hard and making big tackles. I didn't fit that mould. They got behind me, and appreciated what I was trying to do. But, if I'm honest, I struggled to make the desired impact at Racing. Being faced with the threat of relegation didn't help. And neither did missing a penalty against Boca Juniors.

Hugo Gatti was a goalkeeper more familiarly known as *el Loco* Gatti. That tag – meaning 'the Crazy One' – has, down the years, been attached to a number of South American players whose approach to life is a little unconventional. Gatti may not have always thought before he spoke – once, in a newspaper interview on the eve of a match against Argentinos Juniors, he called the precocious Diego Maradona *Gordo* ('Fatty'); the young Diego responded by slamming four goals past him – but what he could do was save spot kicks. That was his speciality. Not that he had to be especially adept at saving penalties to keep out my effort. A slide down the table meant that winning our home matches was imperative – a situation that made for some tense afternoons at Racing's *Estadio Juan Domingo Perón*. On this occasion Boca were leading 1-0 when the award of a penalty gave us a perfect opportunity to draw level. I stepped forward to take it but my attempt was pretty tame. Gatti saved easily. When that kind of thing happens you can only hope that the miss proves to be immaterial, and that the team registers a positive result regardless of your failure. Unfortunately, this was not one of those occasions. There was no salvaging act, no dramatic comeback to bail me out. Boca won 3-0. I went straight home after the match, which was played on a Sunday, and did not reappear from my apartment until I went in for training on the Tuesday. I just couldn't face the backlash.

Our results at the time were not acceptable for a club of Racing's stature and ambition. But what has to be taken into account is the standard of the Argentine league back then, which was unbelievably high. Apart from Mario Kempes, who was playing for Valencia in Spain, all the best Argentine players were playing in Argentina. It was so competitive. All the teams were strong and all the stadiums were full every week. It was a tough year for Racing. The fans were not slow in letting the players know that and, as the team's most extravagant acquisition, I felt their wrath as much as anyone. So too did my family. The team was running out of games to save itself from the drop when Gimnasia y Esgrima La Plata visited Racing's Avellaneda home and left with a 2-0 victory. The Racing supporters were absolutely furious. A group of around 100–150 of them gathered outside after the game to vent their anger in the direction of the players. The most sensible option for us was to remain in the dressing room until they dispersed, which they did after an hour or two. Only then was it safe to come out.

Unfortunately for my mother and Cristina, who had attended the match, they had no such refuge. They were sat in my car in the car park when the rampaging supporters spotted them. Recognising their association with me, the mob swarmed around the car and began rocking it in an attempt to overturn the vehicle. Cristina and my mother were terrified. Thankfully, the intervention of several police officers cut short their ordeal. Goodness knows what the reaction would have been like that season had the club actually suffered relegation, which we eventually managed to avoid.

After hitting the heights in 1976, the following year had, on the whole, been a disappointing one for me. I was hoping for better things in 1978.

Chapter Five
THE DIRTY WAR

T here was complete silence as César Luis Menotti stood in front of 25 hopeful players grouped together in the centre circle of a training pitch at *la Quinta Salvatore,* on a damp May morning in 1978. Our training camp in the town of Jose C Paz had been home for the previous four months, but for three of those in attendance *el Flaco* Menotti was about to bring their stay to an end; his World Cup squad could accommodate 22 players and no more.

For many of the group the imminent announcement was a mere formality. For others – those not so certain of making the final cut – the wait was unbearably tense. I fell into the latter category. One year earlier Menotti had made public a list of 15 players who would definitely be joining him at the World Cup, and my name was on it. That didn't mean I could relax though. It wasn't quite that simple. I had spent the previous three weeks sidelined by injury, and feared the worst as Menotti prepared to wield the axe. Especially when one of those players competing for my position in the squad was an extraordinary 17-year-old called Diego Armando Maradona.

"This has been a difficult decision for me," Menotti informed us. I held my breath. "Lito Bottaniz, Humberto

Bravo . . . and Diego Maradona have not made it." I'd never felt so relieved.

There were several high-quality players who did make that squad but none were so consistently impressive on the training pitch as Maradona. Even though he had still to reach his 18th birthday when the World Cup came around, his secret had been out long before then. He was the little boy who used to entertain the crowd during the half-time break at Argentinos Juniors matches, going through his full repertoire of tricks in front of an enchanted audience. The ball didn't touch the floor in the ten minutes he was out there. Even when the players emerged from the dressing rooms to resume the main event fans chanted "Que se quede!" ("Let him stay!") in support of the performing kid.

Diego was a phenomenon. He had an agent at a very young age, and made his senior debut for Argentinos Juniors when he was just 15 years old. I played against him soon after that. His build was distinctive even then – short and stocky – and he was deceptively strong too. He was left-sided but played 'free' behind the strikers in the classic number-10 position. He was often the talk of the opposing dressing room. We used to say that he had eyes in the back of his neck because whenever you went to put pressure on him he would sense your presence without even looking, take one touch and be gone.

I really treasured the time I spent training with Diego. I loved it. You could set him any challenge, ask him to execute any trick, and he would perfect it within ten minutes. We would sometimes stand alongside each other at the edge of the penalty area with a bunch of balls and attempt to chip them against the crossbar which, in those days, was square-shaped. I was pleased if I hit the target three or four times out of ten, and even then it would clip the top edge of the bar and fly over the goal, or ricochet directly down off its underside. Diego hardly ever missed. He hardly ever had to move to retrieve his ball either, thanks to his remarkable precision; he could place the ball smack against the square face of the crossbar, so it bounced straight back to his feet.

Another popular exercise was a 'keep-ball' drill called *loquito* that involved a ring of players passing the ball between themselves while two in the middle (usually the last two to arrive for training) were assigned the unenviable task of intercepting it. When one of the middle pair did get something on the ball, then the player on the outside who relinquished possession went into the middle himself, along with the (suitably miffed) person standing next to him. For the two in the middle a simple strategy was required – tear about furiously until you made contact with the ball; an extended stay in the middle was a humiliating experience, especially when each pass became accompanied by a chorus of "Olé!" The only time that plan had to be amended was when Diego received the ball. That's when the two runners in the middle would stop, as if someone had hit a pause button. It was an open admission that attempting to relieve Diego of possession was an impossible exercise. Approaching him would only end in embarrassment, via a flick of the ball over the head, or through the legs. Only when Diego released the ball did the chase resume.

It couldn't have been an easy decision to leave out a player of such obvious promise – and one held in such affectionate regard by the public – but Menotti was concerned about the emotional impact that such an enormous event could have on the teenage Maradona. He was deemed unready, and although he has since admitted that he "knew it was coming", the confirmation of his omission was devastating for Diego, who left the camp immediately, as did Humberto Bravo. Lito Bottaniz, on the other hand, accepted Menotti's offer to remain with the group despite his non-inclusion in the official squad. If someone then had predicted that Maradona would play at the next four World Cups – as he did, winning one (1986) and reaching the final in another (1990) – none of us would have argued. His potential was impossible to overlook.

Excluding Maradona in 1978 was a brave move, but any arguments over the decision were rendered irrelevant a few months later when Menotti led Argentina to glory. On a personal level, winning that World Cup was an experience that filled me with contrasting emotions. It still does to this day, albeit for different reasons now.

My status as a world champion is one of which I'm immensely proud. To triumph on home soil, and witness at first hand the unbridled joy that sweeps an entire nation following such a victory, was genuinely thrilling; at the same time, my limited involvement in our historic success – which amounted to a couple of substitute appearances, due partly to a pre-tournament injury inflicted upon me in training by none other than Osvaldo Ardiles – made it difficult for me to feel like anything other than a fringe figure as the whole of Argentina celebrated.

Furthermore, my pride at achieving the ultimate ambition of any footballer has been tinged a little over the ensuing years due to a sinister political undertone that, for some, has tarnished the event – our World Cup triumph boosted the prestige of the brutal military regime that ruled Argentina at the time. I can honestly say that, back then, I was completely unaware of the barbaric events happening – in secret – around us. The situation has been well documented since but, in 1978, was not apparent to a naive young man focused solely on playing football.

I won't delve too deeply into the history of Argentina and its politics, but the situation at that time had such a telling impact on society that I feel some kind of basic explanation is necessary. I'll begin with the events of 24th March 1976, a landmark day on which General Jorge Rafael Videla led a military coup that saw Isabel Perón deposed as leader and Videla assume power as the president of Argentina. It was a move that initially received widespread support in Argentina. That seems remarkable now, considering the subsequent conduct of Videla and his cruel regime. But, at the time of the coup, the people of Argentina were desperate for change. The country was in a complete mess. Isabel Perón had taken office following the death of her husband Juan Domingo Perón in 1974 and her reign had been riddled with problems, chiefly the struggle to contain a fight between the left- and right-wing factions within her own government. Beyond that, guerrilla organisations such as the ERP (the People's Revolutionary Army) were intent on ushering in communist rule, while the Montoneros – the disaffected wing of Peron's administration – were equally intent on unseating the government by any means necessary. The ongoing battle between these rebel groups and the military – 'the Dirty War' – was a violent conflict in which bombings, kidnappings and assassinations were rife. Also, the country had reached a state of catastrophe economically, with a complete lack of order or discipline afflicting society. A shift in power, regardless of who instigated it almost, was welcomed by the majority.

Videla took charge and immediately termed his government *el Proceso*, or the 'the National Reorganisation Process'. All subversives would be suppressed, the nation was informed. What followed was one of the most controversial and inhumane periods in Argentine history. The brutality demonstrated throughout that time cost thousands of people their lives, many of them innocent civilians. That volatile political backdrop is, to this day, also responsible for tainting Argentina's World Cup triumph of 1978.

In March 1976 I was 23 years old. I didn't know anything about politics really. I was a footballer. I was educated to a point, but my entire world revolved around football. That goes for many young men I suppose, not just those who play the game professionally. I didn't pay a great deal of attention to political matters. Having said that, the location of my club during this unsettling time meant that a seriously hostile situation was impossible to ignore.

I was playing in Tucumán, an area where the Dirty War was at its height. The region's terrain, with its dense jungle, provided a perfect base for the warring guerrillas. There was no escaping the political situation in Tucumán. Most of the fighting took place in the jungle, as the military attempted to destroy their opposition at source, but the conflict sometimes spilled into the city as well. This is where the military went to extraordinary lengths to limit the spread of unrest. A series of road blocks were put in place to prevent any rebels with sinister intentions from infiltrating the city. Whole streets were closed off so that guerrillas could not use car bombs as a form of attack. Those kind of explosive strikes were rarely made in public places though. The objective was often to send out a firm warning to the government more than anything else. Direct assassination attempts on leading figures, however, were not uncommon. As a result, the whole transport network around ministerial buildings and the police headquarters was shut down.

All these measures made for such a tense climate. It was a really restrictive environment. There were so many control points along the roads. Whenever I was driving in Tucumán it was guaranteed that my vehicle would be stopped and searched at some point. Every single day. It was the same for everyone. Army officials would ask to see some form of identification and check my driving documents before rummaging around the boot of the car. All the time this was happening another member of the military would be standing around 20 yards away with a gun trained on me, just in case I made any sudden, suspicious movements. In Tucumán I could feel the military presence at all times.

Night-time was the most frightening time in Tucumán. That was when the authorities imposed a curfew. "If you are out on the streets after 11 o'clock in the evening," we were told, "then the state will no longer be responsible for your safety." Say no more. Strolling around town after dark was most definitely not recommended. I must say, I never witnessed any atrocities at first hand. But the sound of bombs exploding during the night offered a constant reminder of the potential dangers lurking right on my doorstep.

The most controversial aspect of Videla's regime was the barbaric, often indiscriminate manner in which they set about erasing their enemy. They didn't just advance into the jungle to wipe out the guerrillas. The net was spread much further afield than that. Anyone who was suspected of siding with the guerrilla movement was in grave danger. Even those with the most tenuous potential links or affiliation, which could simply mean having left-wing tendencies. Those identified as posing a possible threat to the regime were ruthlessly eliminated, and became known as *los Desaparecidos* – 'the Disappeared'.

It's impossible to put an exact figure on the number of people who were 'disappeared' but some estimates imply that 30,000 lives were lost during the conflict. In 1985, two years after military rule came to an end, Videla was convicted of crimes against humanity. At the time, however, the spree of kidnapping, torture and murder was very much a covert operation. With many scared to speak out against the junta for fear of reprisals, and with that same junta controlling the media's output, it was a while before the full extent of the savagery became clear to the public. As it did, the sweeping military offensive left many living in fear. Students, social workers, journalists and teachers were all at risk, with the junta suspecting a large number of guerrilla sympathisers within those sectors of society. Many people were terrified. Cristina's family, for example, burned all books they had relating to Marxism or the history of Russia – anything that may have been deemed left-wing material and would have portrayed them as favouring the 'enemy'.

I didn't personally know anyone who vanished but one of the teachers from Cristina's school in Roque Pérez disappeared. He actually came from a nearby town called Lobos. Cristina had left school by the time he disappeared, but she was told about the incident by her sister's friends who were still pupils there. This teacher was there one day but not the next. Or the day after that, or the day after that, and so on. He just didn't turn up. The school was fed an official line that no one was quite sure where he'd gone. But the fact that he was a known communist led to suspicions that his disappearance could be permanent.

In terms of my own personal safety I would have to say that I was nearer the low-risk end of the scale. The military's bid to quell the opposition in urban areas was highly secretive, so the last thing they wanted was the widespread public intrigue that would have been triggered by the disappearance of a high-profile figure like a professional footballer. Besides, I wasn't one to voice my political beliefs back then. I didn't *have* any political beliefs back then. To a large extent football transcended the political situation. Supporters got behind their team, regardless of their political persuasion, and the stadiums were still full. That was due in no small part to the impending World Cup, which was to be hosted by Argentina for the first time and created a huge sense of excitement all over the country.

Throughout the build-up to the World Cup in 1978, and during the tournament too, César Luis Menotti made a specific effort to separate politics from football. "We love the Argentine people and that's who we are playing for" was his message. Ironically, Menotti was in fact quite a political character himself. His beliefs in that field, which he never attempted to keep secret, placed him on the opposite side of the political fence to the military junta. Had he not already been in charge when the military assumed power in 1976 then it's unlikely that he would have been given the job. He wasn't the regime's preferred choice. More to the point, had he not held the esteemed position of national team boss then his political persuasion could have placed his very existence in danger. Going into exile may have been his only option. But, as long as the team was producing positive results, Menotti was safe in his position. He saw the World Cup as an opportunity to make the people happy during an otherwise difficult time. For us to do that we had to forget about the social climate, he said. Menotti stressed to his players that the only way we could maximise our potential and be successful was to focus 100 per cent on football and nothing else. We could only concern ourselves with the likes of Platini, Bettega, Krol and Neeskens. Not any political figures over whom we had no control.

It seems incredible now that so many people could have 'disappeared' under the military regime. A question I have been asked many times since is why was nothing done to stop the rising number of *los Desaparecidos*. First of all, what has to be understood is that all the official information we received was via the radio, television and newspapers. The ruling junta controlled all of these media outlets, so they had the power to dupe society, which is effectively what they did. We would hear on the news about the fight against the guerrillas, supposedly far away from the cities and towns. The guerrillas were portrayed as the villains and we were made to feel threatened by their presence. A sense of fear was instilled in us, with the military building up its role as our great protector. The guerrillas were the cause of all the trouble, we were led to believe. "But don't worry – the military will save you." That was the junta's message. It was a similar story when it came to disputes like the Cold War. According to all sources of information in Argentina, the US were the good guys and the Russians were the bad guys. It's only when you get older that you recognise this sort of practice as an attempt to brainwash the people, and that things are not that simple. You become more educated, more informed and more aware of what's happening in the world.

There was no freedom of the press in Argentina while the military ruled. I never heard a single dissenting voice on the radio, or read any newspaper comments that objected to the methods of the ruling regime. As a result we were left with a heavily skewed version of events. I'm not saying the guerrillas were passive bystanders in all of this. They fought hard too. But the military were so harsh in their approach.

My then indifference to politics, combined with the distorted nature of the news reports we were being fed, meant that I genuinely wasn't aware of the atrocities that were going on around me. That began to change in early 1977, though, when I flew to Spain to play for Argentina in a tournament that marked the 75th anniversary of Real Madrid. That trip made every one of our travelling party acutely aware that something wasn't quite right.

In those days there were no retractable tunnels through which you exited a plane. Everyone walked down the steps to ground level and then made their way into the airport. When we stepped off the plane in Madrid our focus was immediately drawn to a crowd of people gathered on the airport terrace above us. It wasn't just the mass of people who captured our attention, but what they were holding. Many were brandishing placards, big cards with slogans written on them in Spanish such as "What about the Disappeared?" and "There's no freedom in Argentina". There were more people waiting to greet us as we passed through customs. We were shocked, especially after stopping for a few moments to talk with the protesters. Many were Argentine exiles who had fled to Spain in order to escape Videla and his fearsome regime. Some of them had family or friends who had disappeared. Our team officials tried to assure us that the people at the airport were lying, attempting to undermine the prestige of our country ahead of the World Cup, but we weren't convinced. Why would they go to such lengths to display their anguish if they didn't genuinely feel that way? I wondered just what was happening in my country. That episode put the first seed of doubt in my mind.

One of the main reasons why that experience in Madrid was so startling was that, up to that point, we'd never witnessed anything like it in Argentina. The potential consequences were too serious. But gradually the severity of the situation dawned on the public and action was taken. In April 1977 a group of women whose children had disappeared began to meet in Buenos Aires every week and marched around the Plaza de Mayo. They demanded answers. Steadily the number of protesters grew, as *las Madres de la Plaza de Mayo* became a symbol of courage and defiance. These highly visible demonstrations attracted much attention, bringing the plight of *los Desaparecidos* into the public's consciousness. After that, support for the military regime began to diminish. And quickly.

Regardless of events off the pitch, Menotti's preparation for the World Cup was meticulous. A provisional squad of 24 players was summoned to the national team's training camp – *la Concentración* – around four months before the start of the tournament. Despite the absence of so many leading players the domestic league in Argentina was still contested that year (it kicked off in March), as clubs released their star men without any great resistance. It's impossible to imagine such a situation occurring nowadays. Our squad size increased to 25 following the arrival of *el Matador* Mario Kempes, the Valencia striker permitted to join up late because he was the only one amongst us who was playing for a European club.

For me, incidentally, the World Cup wasn't the only major event in which I participated in 1978. In fact (just in case my wife is reading this) winning the tournament was merely the second most memorable thing that happened to me that year. On 21st January 1978 I married Cristina.

I'll never forget the first time I saw Cristina. Before I continue, I must say I'm fully aware that a statement of that kind can lead to a barrage of mickey-taking for a footballer. Or an ex-footballer. Football players are not the most romantic of types. But the memory of that first encounter with my wife really is that vivid.

It was in the bakery in Roque Pérez. I was 17 and she was 14. Just as I was walking out she was walking in. We passed in the doorway, glancing at each other as we did so. I took one look at her and thought, "Wow!" She was such a beautiful girl. I was pretty scared of women at that point, so not so much as a word was exchanged. But what an impression she made on me. And, I later found out, the feeling was mutual. Just recently Cristina recalled the incident when we were amongst some friends. She said – and I quote – "When I saw Ricky for the first time he made an instant impact. I was so impressed by this tall, long-haired guy. I thought to myself, 'I'm going to marry that man'." It's true!

About a year after that meeting in the bakery I was playing for the Roque Pérez representative team. Although I was unaware of the connection at the time, Cristina's father was the team masseur. Every time I went for a massage the other boys would say, "We know exactly why you're going for another rub-down . . . you want to get close to his daughter." I'd never seen his daughter – or at least I didn't think I'd ever seen his daughter – but from what my teammates were saying I thought she must be special.

The next time I actually saw Cristina was a while later, at a local dance. My children howl with laughter whenever I recall the way those old-fashioned social gatherings in Roque Pérez used to work. I must admit, it was all quite primitive. The dances were usually held in the bar of a tennis club or football club. The girls used to sit around the edge of the room while the boys congregated in the middle. The process by which the boys asked the girls to dance was pretty terrifying really. If you saw a girl you liked the custom was to catch her eye and simply nod in her direction. No need for conversation. This was courting, Roque Pérez style. If the girl accepted the invitation she would step forward, and the boy would exhale a huge sigh of relief.

If the girl rejected your advance, then you had problems. Sometimes a girl would pretend she couldn't see you when you offered a "Would-you-like-to-dance-with-me?" nod, glancing up, down and anywhere else in the room as she tried her best to avoid making eye contact. Other times the girl might say, "Er . . . no thanks . . . I don't like this song" and then moments later she'd be dancing to the same tune with someone else. It was soul-destroying for many a young man. Another constant danger was that the less popular girls were desperate for attention. They jumped out of their seats in response to anything remotely resembling a nod that was aimed vaguely in their direction, even if it was clearly intended for the more attractive girl sat next to them. Suddenly you'd be shuffling around the dance floor with a big – albeit grateful – girl whom you hadn't even asked to dance with in the first place. And all that while your friends stood behind her giggling. What an ordeal.

I actually danced with Cristina's sister, María Ester, once or twice (she wasn't one of those who stepped up uninvited; I asked her to dance). I couldn't help but enquire after her sister though. She told me that Cristina was at home, although I did see her occasionally when she came with her aunt to pick up Maria. Then, one night, there she was! We finally got to dance, and the rest is history. It certainly wasn't my dancing skills that clinched the deal but, whatever it was, we've been together ever since.

The wedding was in Roque Pérez and thousands of people congregated outside the church. When I stepped out of the car on arrival I found myself surrounded by a throng of well-wishers, patting me on the back and pulling at my jacket. I could barely move. It was chaos. The event generated so much attention. I was a well-known footballer playing at one of the country's biggest clubs and also for the national team. With the World Cup approaching, any activity a potential squad member engaged in automatically became big news. It seemed as though the whole town had turned out.

It was a wonderful occasion, but my focus soon turned back to football. After a honeymoon of around 20 days not far from the coastal resort of Mar del Plata I was off to la Concentración. Cristina still jokes about how I married her and then immediately abandoned my new wife to live with a bunch of men for several months. But this was no time for romance . . . we had a World Cup to win!

I had gradually managed to establish myself in the national team thanks to the trust shown in me by a great man who was like a father figure to me: Menotti. To understand how difficult it was for someone playing outside the capital to gain international recognition you first have to appreciate the sheer vastness of Argentina, as well as the powerful hold that Buenos Aires has long had over Argentine football.

Argentina is the eighth largest country on the planet, with a land mass of around 2.7 million square kilometres. The whole of England could fit into it 20 times. If the national team manager wished to assess, at first hand, a player of inter-national potential then he would have to travel great distances at no small expense if that player was way up north in Tucumán, for example, just as I was. Likewise, any player selected from the far reaches of the country was faced with a similar challenge in getting to the capital. With so many clubs based in Buenos Aires the national team was for so long dominated by players from Boca, River Plate, Independiente, San Lorenzo and Racing. Why bother looking elsewhere for talent when there was such a rich array of it localised around the capital? That was the traditional way of thinking. If your club did not fall within the confines of the city it was a case of out of sight, out of mind. It was like playing in a different country. Your name would hardly feature in the newspapers. That, however, all changed when Menotti took over.

Hailing from Rosario, and nicknamed *el Flaco* ('the Thin One') because of his slender frame, Menotti shot to promi-nence in 1973 by leading Huracán to the Metropolitano title at the age of just 34. Such was his standing in the game that he went on to manage Barcelona in the 1980s, with his spell in charge at the Nou Camp preceding that of Terry Venables.

Menotti's greatest success though, came as boss of Argentina. He was appointed in place of Vladislao Cap, a former Racing player who represented Argentina at the 1962 World Cup. Cap had overseen a disappointing 1974 World Cup campaign in which Argentina lost three of their six matches, including a 4-0 thumping at the hands of Johan Cruyff's Holland. Cap himself had been hastily brought in when a row between previous incumbent Omar Sívori and the Argentine Football Association had left the coach's position vacant shortly before the tournament began. That followed on from 1970, when Argentina failed to even qualify for the finals in Mexico, while fierce rivals Brazil romped to victory. The Argentine Football Association (AFA) were desperate to see Argentina compete alongside the very best, and Menotti was the man entrusted with the task of making it happen.

One of many qualities that Menotti demonstrated during the build-up to the World Cup was his willingness to use players based outside the capital. It was an approach that went against tradition, and one that struggled to gain support from a Buenos Aires-biased press. It was a brave move, but one that I, and many others on the outskirts, welcomed. The *Selección del Interior* was a team consisting of players chosen from non-Buenos Aires clubs (the 'Interior' in Argentina refers to everywhere but Buenos Aires). It expanded the potential pool of players from which Menotti would select his final squad, effectively opening up the country in footballing terms. It wasn't the full national side, but the team did represent Argentina abroad. In 1974, I represented the *Selección del Interior* on a three-week tour that included games in Brazil, Bolivia and at home in Argentina too.

More pertinently perhaps, Menotti instigated a change in

style. A different mindset. It wasn't like he was preaching something entirely new. More a reinvention of an old ideal. To help you understand what I mean by that I must first explain how football has evolved in Argentina over the years.

Throughout the history of the game in my country there has coexisted two contrasting football philosophies. To begin with there was *la Nuestra*. Translating to 'Our Style', *la Nuestra* is a term that was coined by Argentinians to describe the exuberant way in which they played the game in the 1930s and 1940s. To adopt the principles of *la Nuestra* was to place the onus on attack, to play with expression and flamboyance. Nutmegs, feints, dummies. Fancy tricks. It wasn't quick or direct – there was no rush to get forward. Exponents of *la Nuestra* took their time. Going straight for the kill wasn't the objective. The emphasis was on entertainment. It was an approach that characterised Argentinian football for many years and spawned some wonderful players like Alfredo di Stéfano, one of the all-time greats who went on to inspire Real Madrid's early domination of the European Cup.

Argentina and its leading clubs, exhibiting what they claimed was their very own brand of dazzling football, enjoyed some success during this period. The problem was, the national team wasn't really tested, not outside of South America anyway. Argentina, runners-up at the first ever World Cup in 1930, did not participate in the competition between 1934 and 1954. In that time, they hardly faced opposition from any continent other than their own. They didn't come up against an array of styles or teams that were capable of nullifying their swaggering approach. They didn't suffer any crushing defeats that may have forced them to rethink, or question the validity of *la Nuestra*. There was no need to make any alterations. Or so they thought.

That all changed after the 1958 World Cup. That tournament, held in Sweden, provided Argentinian football with a shuddering wake-up call, and is widely regarded as being a major turning point in the history of our football. What didn't help Argentina's cause was the loss of three key players shortly before the event. *Oriundi* is a term given to players of Italian descent who were born in Argentina but returned to the land of their ancestors to experience the glamour of Serie A in their peak years. Omar Sívori, Humberto Maschio and Antonio Angelillo, known collectively as 'the Angels with Dirty Faces', were three such examples. They were Argentina internationals – and good ones at that – before they left for Italy in 1957, acquiring Italian citizenship soon after.

Even without the *Oriundi* Argentina could not have anticipated the humiliation they were to suffer in Sweden. In their final group game they were dealt an embarrassing 6-1 thrashing by Czechoslovakia. It was a scoreline that represented the team's heaviest ever defeat, and one that would not be repeated for another 50-odd years. The Czechs were dominant in every department. Most notably, Argentina were made to look slow and cumbersome against a side of far superior speed and stamina. The people of Argentina were ashamed of their team's feeble showing, as the players found out for themselves when they returned to a hostile reception at Buenos Aires airport. Things had to improve.

That shameful display in 1958 effectively signalled the end of *la Nuestra*. The national team's failure sparked a furious reaction that was reflected in dwindling attendances at subsequent domestic matches due to a mixture of disappointment and disillusionment among fans. The game suffered a real slump and something had to change. The answer was to adopt a more defensive, organised, 'European' approach: the opposite of *la Nuestra* in fact. Out went risk-taking and in came a heightened fear of losing. All of a sudden winning was everything. A man named Osvaldo Zubeldía was at the forefront of this revolution. He was the coach of Estudiantes and implemented a tough training regime that, up to that point, had been a completely foreign concept in Argentina. Zubeldía was highly tactical, and introduced a variety of new ideas to the Argentinian game. His team pressed the opposition when they didn't have the ball, rather than sit back and allow them to advance. They worked diligently on perfecting the offside trap, and spent hours practising set pieces. *La Nuestra* this most definitely wasn't.

In terms of getting results, Zubeldía's methods worked. In the late 1960s Estudiantes were crowned club champions of South America and then the world. But it wasn't just 'winning football' they were playing; the desperate desire to achieve success had sinister consequences for Argentine football. And there were none more sinister than Estudiantes. Their violent clash with Manchester United in 1968, for the title of club world champions, is best remembered for a series of nasty fouls, callous assaults and sending-offs. By the time Estudiantes faced AC Milan in the same competition 12 months later, the Argentinian people were growing tired of what had become known as *anti-fútbol*.

Even for a nation steeped in the tradition of *viveza*, this type of behaviour was unacceptable. *Viveza* is a word used to describe an act of cunning, or quick-thinking. Something crafty. A demonstration of *viveza* is generally applauded in Argentina. I know that English people will not thank me for saying this, but Diego Maradona's 'Hand of God' goal against

England in 1986 is a prime example of *viveza*. Some would call it cheating of course. Even so, the conduct of Estudiantes in the 1960s was stretching things way beyond the boundaries.

After AC Milan were subjected to such a violent onslaught that three Estudiantes players were imprisoned in 1969, things came to a head. Failure to make the World Cup in 1970 only added to the unrest among football followers, and out of that dismay emerged an air of nostalgia. There was a longing for a return of *la Nuestra*. In Menotti they had just the man for the job. He was something of an artist, with a romantic ideal when it came to football. He understood the importance of winning. But he also reasoned that only one club can claim the championship title, so if the other teams in the division can't be winners then they must at least give the fans something – entertainment. Menotti restored a sense of freedom to Argentinian football. He revived the concept of *la Nuestra*. Not in its purest form; he sent the team's physical trainer Ricardo Pizzarotti on a European mission in order to pick up new ideas and improve conditioning. And his sides were defensively well drilled, so it wasn't a case of all-out attack as it was in the old days. But it was certainly more *la Nuestra* than *anti-fútbol*.

Menotti was an outstanding manager. Not just in the way he approached the game, but the way in which he treated his players. He was always fair, he always defended us in the press and, like all the great managers, he knew how best to deal with each individual in order to optimise their ability. I witnessed for myself a perfect example of his clever man management in the March of 1976. The national team was about to embark on a tour of Eastern Europe to play the USSR, Poland and Hungary, and I was summoned to the

AFA headquarters in Buenos Aires. I assumed the purpose of the trip was to receive notice of my inclusion in the squad for the impending tour. Why else would I have been flown in from Tucumán? The news I received on arriving in Buenos Aires was not of an international call-up, though. Precisely the opposite, in fact. "I'm not taking you to Europe," Menotti informed me, as we sat together in the AFA office. "But I will definitely keep you in mind."

At first I didn't know whether to feel up or down. But I soon realised that Menotti wouldn't have gone to such great lengths to reassure me, in person, that I was in his plans if he didn't mean it. My confidence soared. Along with confirmation that I was in his thoughts Menotti promised me I would be involved in the next international tour. That was the following year, when Argentina were invited to play Real Madrid at the Bernabeu. Sure enough, Menotti was true to his word. He was always true to his word. I went to Madrid.

I remember another occasion when Menotti was asked a question about me in a press conference. I couldn't believe it when I read his response. "Villa is an excellent header of the ball," he said. An excellent header of the ball? I thought he'd got the wrong player. Anyone who saw me play knows that heading was never my strongest asset. It wasn't really an asset at all. I wanted the ball at my feet. That's when I was in the game. The reason Menotti made such a public declaration was, he later admitted, to lift my confidence. It was another example of how he never stopped thinking of ways to get more out of his players, even if I'm not completely convinced that the episode did actually improve my heading; that area of weakness was always going to take more than a few encouraging words from the manager to rectify.

Menotti was constantly challenging his players. If, in training, one of us successfully executed a nutmeg, or *caño* as we call it, he would say, "Well done. But it's one thing doing it on the training pitch. I bet you don't have the courage to try it on match day, when 60,000 people are watching." He wanted a positive reaction, and applauded you when he got it. Players were encouraged to go looking for the ball, and not to hide. Menotti was very logical. He would instruct us to attack the spaces out wide and, if that route became congested, to move the ball back inside and explore a different avenue. At the back, we wouldn't have four defenders marking one opposing striker – the spare men in defence were given sufficient freedom to move forward and join in the play.

Every aspect of the game was covered, to prepare the team for all possibilities. Menotti wanted his side to play attractive football, but also demanded a high work rate. Allowing opponents to run beyond you and failing to track back was never acceptable, and if one of your teammates slipped over – one of the fullbacks, for instance – a colleague was expected to fill in for him. He told us that when he looked at a photo of his team conceding a goal he wanted to see every single one of his players in view sprawled out on the floor, straining every muscle in a desperate bid to prevent the opposition from scoring.

The final preparations in 1978 were conducted at *la Concentración*. Menotti believed the most effective way of keeping players' minds focused solely on winning the World Cup was to confine them to a training camp. There were no distractions to tempt the easily led – and we had a few of those among us – and no interference from outside. Nothing but football. Even the conversation revolved around football most of the time. One topic players rarely covered around the dinner table was politics. Ossie was probably the most formally educated individual in the squad and he kept a keen eye on current affairs, but the there was little interest in the subject elsewhere in the camp.

While Menotti's instruction to think only of football was accepted by all it was impossible to completely ignore the state of tension that had engulfed the country. The guerrillas would have gained nothing by launching an attack on the nation's football team. On the contrary, such a manoeuvre would have left them with a seriously depleted level of support. So we never felt threatened ourselves. But there were fears amongst the authorities that the rebels may somehow attempt to disturb the tournament in a bid to gain publicity, so the security presence that surrounded us – and the competition in general – was a 24-hour operation.

In *la Concentración* our movements were closely monitored. Whenever we returned to the camp after a day off or a weekend at home each car had to pass through the entrance to the complex individually. We had to park some distance away from the main building and walk in. Every bag we had was checked for suspicious items, and the same went for any of our visitors. After a while we got to know the guards and they became more relaxed about the whole thing. Everywhere the squad went we were shadowed. When we briefly switched to the Villa Marista training camp in Mar del Plata there was an armed patrolman on each corner of our hotel block. Nothing was left to chance.

One of the first things Menotti did at *la Concentración* was inform us of the rooming arrangements. Each room on the complex was to be occupied by two players, with none of the squad having a say in who they would share with for the next four months. Menotti's approach work was so precise, he even studied the players' personalities to determine which pairs would be most compatible. The manager stood before us in a small meeting room and revealed the pairings. At the risk of sounding a little overdramatic, the announcement that followed triggered a chain of events that ultimately led to a completely unexpected yet unforgettable chapter in my life. It also changed the course of history for a club 7,000 miles away that, at the time, I didn't even know existed.

Chapter Six
CAMPÉON DEL MUNDO

A little midfielder from Córdoba called Osvaldo Ardiles was my roommate in the months leading up to the 1978 World Cup.

César Luis Menotti, having assessed the whole group, came to the conclusion that the two of us were well suited. A factor in his thinking may have been the strong likelihood that Ossie and I would both be in the starting line-up when the competition eventually kicked off; the alternative of pairing two players who were competing for a similar spot in the team could have led to unnecessary tension. Menotti emphasised that his decision was final. Strictly non-negotiable. I certainly had no problem with that. I was more than happy to room with Ossie. I got along with all the players in the squad. We would sit with each other at dinner and engage in conversation. But that's not to say I could have lived with them all. Sharing living space with some of the players in that group would have been very interesting! While I consider myself and Ossie to have been sensible professionals, others were not quite that way inclined. *Se subian a cualquier colectivo* is the term we use, which basically means they would 'jump on any bus'. In other words, they were easily led astray.

I first met Ossie in 1975 when we were both included in a *Selección del Interior* squad (he was playing in Córdoba at the time). As with most players operating outside the capital, I'd never heard of him up to that point. He was a friendly guy, a family man like me. During the lead-up to the World Cup we obviously spoke a great deal, and became good friends. That, without question, laid the foundations for my move to Tottenham. If I had roomed with any other player then my future would almost certainly have been ushered down a different path.

In April we inherited a third room member, when Mario Kempes joined the camp as the Spanish season came to a close. Our room had a small adjoining area – a bit like a physio's room – and *el Matador*, an easily likeable man, stayed there. As another son of Córdoba he'd known Ossie for some years, playing alongside him at Instituto Atlético Central Córdoba, and the new arrangement worked for everyone. Even when three players were cut from the provisional squad, thus vacating rooms elsewhere, Mario stayed with us.

As a roommate Kempes was fine; as a teammate he was brilliant. What a goalscorer. When he arrived at *la Concentración* he had just claimed 28 league goals for Valencia to finish the campaign as top scorer in Spain for the second season running. Goalscoring is so often about form and confidence, and Mario was peaking in both.

Kempes was among a clutch of top-class individuals in and around the final squad, including several who specialised in the same role as I did. To be honest, there was such competition for the number 10 spot that I was just happy to make the cut. Argentina was blessed with an abundance of talent in that 'free' position. Maradona missed out but Norberto

Alonso of River Plate, a wonderfully creative, elegant left-footer, was included. He wore the number 1 shirt, because of an unusual system that saw the squad numbered in alphabetical order (I was number 22, at the other end of the line). Ricardo Bochini was another vying for my position. He was a great player, but he drifted a little and seemed to save his best performances for his club Independiente, where he is revered above all others to this day. *El Bocha* was also excluded by Menotti in 1978.

I nearly missed out too, thanks to Ossie of all people. As part of our preparations we played a training match on a brand new pitch at Vélez Sarsfield, a few weeks before the final squad was announced. During the game the ball dropped between me and Ossie and we both challenged for it. I got there first (I always said I was quicker than Ossie) and flicked it up. Ossie lost his footing, though, slipping on the new surface and accidentally hit me with a two-footed lunge that left me with a gashed shin. I had the wound stitched but suffered a further setback when it became infected. The team doctor, Chacho Fort, was already under pressure following a series of errors. This was to be his last one, though, because he was sacked after failing to treat my injury correctly. Chacho's time was up. I was just hoping it didn't spell the end of my World Cup involvement too.

In total I was sidelined for about 20 days, which included a week away from *la Concentración* while I struggled to even walk. Eventually I managed to shake off the effects of the original injury, the infection and an unwelcome bout of diarrhoea as well. Thankfully, Menotti kept faith in me. He resisted the option of selecting a fully fit alternative, much to my relief. Having said that, missing a crucial stage of the build-up through injury had seriously diminished my chances of lining up from the start of our opening game against Hungary.

In the first stage we won 2-1 against both Hungary and France, before losing 1-0 to Italy. That meant we finished second behind the Italians, thus qualifying for the next round of matches where we were grouped with Poland, Brazil and Peru. The two second-phase group winners were to be rewarded with a place in the World Cup final.

Failing to finish top of our initial group saw us leave Buenos Aires to play our next series of games in Rosario, a city situated just under 200 miles north-west of the capital. Although it wasn't planned, the move was ideal in many respects. Rosario's *Estadio Cordiviola* could accommodate less than half as many spectators as River Plate's *Monumental* in Buenos Aires, but what it lacked in numbers it more than made up for in noise. The Rosario ground is so tight that the crowd are packed in right up to the pitch, creating a fantastic atmosphere.

Our first opponents in the second phase were Poland. The Poles, who finished third in 1974, weren't quite the force they had been but still boasted a notable band of top-class players. Goalkeeper Jan Tomaszewski had famously frustrated England at Wembley on the way to the previous World Cup, Zbigniew Boniek was a bright young prospect who went on to fulfil his considerable promise at Juventus, and Grzegorz Lato was the tournament's top scorer four years earlier. So a 2-0 victory, with Mario Kempes scoring twice, was an impressive result for us. It was in that game that I made my World Cup debut, as a half-time substitute for Jose Valencia when the score was 1-0. I was satisfied with my contribution. I also made an impact in the next game, when I was again introduced from the bench after 45 minutes. This time I went on in place of

Ossie, in a goalless draw against Brazil. Unfortunately, the impact I made on this occasion wasn't a positive one. I should have been sent off.

I'm still not quite sure how it happened. Just a couple of minutes into the second half the ball bounced between myself and a Brazilian player – Roberto, I think, or maybe Batista – and I lunged for it. Unintentionally, my raised foot made no contact with the ball but instead made contact with my opponent's thigh. It all happened in a flash. A swarm of Brazil players charged up to me and I knew it was a poor challenge. Nowadays it would definitely be deemed a red-card offence. Even then it was deemed a red-card offence. Maybe the fact that I was on the home team helped me avoid an early exit. It wasn't premeditated though. It was the first and last bad foul of my whole career. I wasn't a bad tackler. I wasn't a tackler full stop. I can only think that my emotions got the better of me. It was a crucial World Cup match, we were facing our great rivals, the game was finely poised and the atmosphere was pulsating. The occasion got to me.

It was a moment of madness and one that I immediately regretted. On a lighter note, it did make me aware of the far-reaching impact that such an incident can have, coming as it did in the most visible of settings. I'd heard people talk about the World Cup attracting a global audience, but only when I arrived for my first day of training at Tottenham did I fully appreciate what that meant. Although I was oblivious to it at the time – due to the fact that my grasp of English did not extend much beyond the word *hello* – Steve Perryman made a point of having a quiet word with some of my new colleagues, as they stood around waiting for a five-a-side game to start. More specifically, he was addressing those whom I was about to face. Steve, outstanding captain that he was, felt obliged to warn the lads of the potential danger they were about to encounter. "Just be careful," he stressed, shooting a stern glance in my direction. "This bloke is one nasty bastard."

Steve had watched the World Cup on television that summer. Having seen me commit a terrible foul against Brazil, he was convinced his club had signed an aggressive midfielder, a rugged, tenacious player. It was a description that could not possibly have been further from the truth. We laugh about it now, of course. I barely made a tackle in my time as a footballer, let alone a foul. It's amazing how a player can acquire a reputation in just a split second. But I'm sure it didn't take the boys long to realise that their new signing wasn't quite the ferocious competitor they'd been told to expect.

That 0-0 draw with Brazil meant the two of us led the group, level on three points each with one game still to play. The events that followed prompted a blaze of controversy many years later.

In the final round of matches, played on the same day but at different times, Brazil beat Poland 3-1 in the early kick-off to leave us knowing exactly what we had to do. The brief was simple: beat Peru by four goals and we were in the World Cup final. A simple brief, but a tough assignment. One, however, that we completed successfully; a 6-0 victory saw us pip Brazil to a final showdown with Holland.

The allegations of bribery and corruption that now surround the match have been well documented, with the furore created by our resounding win impossible to ignore. The fact that Peru's goalkeeper Ramón Quiroga was born in Argentina has been the subject of much contention, while others talk of alleged collusion at government level. I'm not naive, but I was there that night. Personally, I don't believe the conspiracy theories.

There are several reasons why I regard our win against Peru as a legitimate triumph. First of all, we were a formidable team, thoroughly prepared in every department and packed full of genuine quality. Completely focused. The identity of our opponents was another factor. We regularly beat Peru – they hadn't got the better of us in nearly ten years leading up to the tournament, and we'd beaten them twice just a few months earlier as part of our World Cup preparations. It's relevant also, I think, to point out that football teams of South American countries have their own distinctive characteristics. Brazil, for instance, are renowned for their attacking flair. Uruguay, in contrast, are traditionally a difficult side to beat, usually tough and defensively well-drilled. Peru, meanwhile, are more in the mould of Brazil (although not as adept), boasting excellent technical players like Teófilio Cubillas. What they didn't do so well was defend. We always sensed we could score goals against them. And, don't forget, Peru's elimination had already been confirmed by the time we played them – losing to both Brazil (0-3) and Poland (0-1) had seen to that – leaving them with nothing meaningful to play for.

I failed to make the match-day squad for the Peru game (it wasn't the case back then that every squad member not in the starting XI took a place on the bench), so my role was reduced to that of a spectator. But I was with the team when Menotti issued his pre-match chat. Everything went according to plan. Menotti stressed the importance of scoring in the first 20 minutes – which we did, through Kempes – and then another by half-time; a request granted by Alberto Tarantini, shortly before the break. On top of all that, the venue was perfect. The stadium in Rosario is notoriously loud, and the home crowd generated a rousing atmosphere.

It was then on to the final in Buenos Aires's *Estadio Monumental*. There, amidst a storm of ticker tape (which, incidentally, remains a popular form of welcome in Argentinian football to this day – kick-off is sometimes delayed while a member of the ground staff walks across the goalmouth armed with a device that blows paper off the pitch) we beat Holland 3-1, after extra-time, to win the World Cup. Again I was privy to the pre-match briefing – when Menotti urged the side to put pressure on our skilful Dutch opponents high up the pitch, in an attempt to keep them a good distance from our goal – but, again, I wasn't named as a substitute.

The whole nation rejoiced. Argentina were world champions for the first time. It was an historic achievement that is embedded in the record books – nobody can ever take that away from us. For some, however, the controversial conduct of the military government under which the tournament was won means that question marks over the validity of the triumph remain.

It can be argued that the feel-good factor instigated by our World Cup victory helped Videla and his military regime extend their term of power. The wave of joy that swept the nation may well have allowed people to forget for a moment the country's crushing economic problems or the ongoing Dirty War that had seen support for the government plummet. Those charged with running the country at that time have since been judged negatively – rightly so – which does leave something of a sour taste. But I can guarantee that their presence did not affect events on the pitch. If there was any suspicious activity surrounding any of our matches then I never saw it.

There were occasions when we came face to face with the government's top men, but it was just for show really. An opportunity for an under-fire regime to gain some positive publicity. Leopoldo Galtieri, for instance, came and visited us at *la Concentración*. Galtieri was a leading official in the military junta at that time and later became president. It was his order, in fact, to invade the Falklands in 1982 – a decision that would have a major impact on my life. In 1978, however, he was operating under Videla. He arrived at the training ground via helicopter, landing right in the middle of the pitch. He addressed the whole squad, wishing us good luck and assuring us that the entire country was behind us. He certainly didn't put any undue pressure on us to be successful.

During Galtieri's visit an open offer was made to every player in the squad: "Would anyone like a helicopter ride?" I declined, but only because I was scared. I would have done almost anything to break free from the monotony of that training camp! Some of the players accepted the invitation and took off for a brief ride. We now accuse those players of being military insiders. Jokingly, of course.

General Videla was not a renowned football fan but he also paid us a visit, entering the dressing room after our victory over Peru in Rosario accompanied by former US Secretary of State Henry Kissinger. I missed out on selection that day so I didn't witness the meeting for myself. I'm not sure that Videla received the warmest of welcomes. It's true to say that footballers are generally quite rebellious against authorities and by 1978 we were all beginning to question the military's approach, even before we'd found out about the Disappeared.

Alberto Tarantini tells a story of how, in the Rosario changing room that day, he subtly displayed his personal disapproval of the country's then-president. Tarantini, who was in the shower when Videla began shaking hands with the players following the match, purposely washed his nether regions before offering Videla his hand. As I said, it's not an incident that I saw myself, but if it's true then Tarantini was a brave man. It has since become quite a famous tale.

After we beat Holland in the final Videla presented the trophy to our captain Daniel Passarella. I've no doubt the junta realised the beneficial effect that a World Cup win would have on its standing. But I will always maintain that we won the World Cup legitimately, fair and square. Not everyone seems to accept that, though, with the contrasting affection afforded to Argentina's World Cup winners of 1978 and 1986 perfectly illustrating that point. The team that Maradona so brilliantly led to victory in '86 is revered in Argentina. More so than the boys of '78. Just recently on television I saw a programme that was paying tribute to Argentina's past World Cup winners. It was completely focused on 1986. I felt like phoning in and asking why we didn't get a mention. Don't forget, there are two stars on that Argentina shirt.

It goes without saying that winning the World Cup filled us with much pride; inadvertently helping to boost the prestige of a barbaric government at the same time most certainly didn't. We were just playing football, with the World Cup our prime target. The subject does, however, still present me with a few awkward moments. Defending my participation in that tournament is sometimes difficult, and never more so than when I meet relatives of *los Desaparecidos*. I often get asked questions along the lines of "How could you represent a country that was responsible for such appalling human rights violations?" Of course I can understand why people pose such questions. But the fact is we genuinely didn't realise how severe the situation was. The Argentine people were suppressed, with those who did suspect serious foul play too scared to speak out. Only years later did the full story unfold. We were a group of young men with a minimal interest in politics. Our lives consisted of football, football and more football. As professionals the ultimate goal for us was to win the World Cup. I was a footballer, not a politician. I wanted to play for my national team – that was my dream. I wanted to win the World Cup. I wanted to improve myself, to be successful. I was unaware of the awful things that were happening around me.

I have since played in benefit matches for those who disappeared. Now fully informed of events, I will always lend my support to *las Madres de la Plaza de Mayo*. We all should. The most difficult question in all of this was put to me once by a mother whose child was among those who disappeared. She asked me, "If you had known what was happening back then would you still have played?" It would have been easy for me to have told her "No". It is now customary to say that we would have refused to play for our country had we been fully aware of the regime's methods. But honestly, hand on heart, I'm not sure that I can answer that question. If I hadn't played then someone else would have taken my place. Could I have made a difference? The World Cup would have been contested regardless. The truth is we didn't have all the information to hand so we didn't have a choice to make. All we wanted to do was win the World Cup for the people of Argentina. The better we performed in the competition,

Menotti kept reminding us, the higher morale would be amongst the public.

In the present day a large number of people are vehemently against the military junta that ruled during that period in Argentine history. At the time, however, the public weren't prepared to voice their dissent. Not everyone fought the regime, and those who were opposed to it kept quiet. They were too terrified to break their silence. Maybe as a society we could have reacted. Although we shouldn't forget that, even if they're reluctant to admit so now, a considerable number of people did support the regime back then. My conscience is clear. I don't feel guilty. I am willing to appear at benefit games for *los Desaparecidos* and talk to relatives of the victims. I'm happy to show my face and take their questions on board. I don't feel as though I have anything to be ashamed of. Unlike in 1978 I can now recognise the issue. Like everyone else, I say, "Nunca más" ('Never again').

That willingness to front up to the issue has led to one or two sticky situations, such as the time when I received an unexpected phone call from a journalist asking me if I would like to attend a function that was being held to commemorate *los Desaparecidos*. It was a kind of debate, or discussion, and I was invited to sit on the panel as a representative of Argentina's 1978 World Cup-winning squad. I've never turned my back on the controversy or tried to avoid it. The media are familiar with my attitude on the subject, hence the invitation to such an event. It was held in a theatre in San Telmo, a neighbourhood of Buenos Aires, with the audience made up of people related to – or otherwise connected to – those who disappeared. I decided to go along. In doing so I ignored the popular advice of those around me. "Why chance it, Ricky?"

The perfect pose! All smiles for the camera
at an early age.

Who needs a bicycle? Where I come from,
we learned to ride horses instead.

On our farm with my father, my sister Noemí and my best friend – la pelota.
I rarely let that ball out of my sight.

On holiday with my mother and Noemí in Mar del Plata. As you can see, I was well fed as a child!

At school as a child. I'm not sure if I ever checked out the location of England on that globe.

Showing my versatility by playing in goal for Santiago Larre U-15s.

No, it's not the actor Christopher Lee! It's me as a teenager on my official identity card.

My first experience of senior football came with Santiago Larre in 1966/67. I'm in the front row, second from the right.

Representing my town Roque Pérez in 1969. That's me in the front row, second from the right. My wife Cristina's father, our masseur, is standing far left.

Just about to make my senior debut for Quilmes at the age of 18, in La Bombonera. I'm in the middle of the front row.

As a young
professional at
Quilmes.

Holding the ball in a team photo with San Martín of Tucumán in 1973.

Fresh faced and clean shaven, as a member of the second division's representative side.

Starring in a 'glamorous' photo-shoot in a Tucumán sugar depot – we were sponsored by the sugar company.

Not letting go of the ball – again – whilst at Atlético Tucumán in 1974.

Scoring my first goal for Atlético Tucumán, July 1974.

Lining up for Argentina's Selección del Interior in 1975. I'm in the front row, third from the left. Recognise the little midfielder on the far left? It's my 'other half', Osvaldo Ardiles.

Playing for Atlético Tucumán, the club at which I enjoyed my most prolific spell as a player; with 68 goals in 108 games I made quite a name for myself.

REVISTA

VILLA, EL HOMBRE DEL MILLON DE DOLARES

CURSOS NO TRADICIONALES PARA CHICOS CON INQUIETUDES

COMO APRENDER A CREAR

NOVIAS, LA MODA MAS FELIZ DEL MUNDO

'Villa, the Million Dollar Man.' My record-breaking move to Racing Club in 1977 was big news.

In the colours of Racing Club, 1977.

The Argentinian national team, 1977. Back row, left to right: Passarella, Gallego, Olguín, Pernía, Gatti, Carrascosa. Front row: Bertoni, Ardiles, Luque, Villa, Larrosa.

With Cristina, my true love.

The most important signature of my life!

Our wedding day, 21st January 1978.

Competing against Zbigniew Boniek during a friendly v Poland in the build-up to the 1978 World Cup.

'Argentina – World Champions 1978'.

Playing against Brazil at the 1978 World Cup.

they said. "They may try to implicate you." But while some felt I was on a hiding to nothing I chose to show up anyway.

I arrived at the venue and took my place on the stage. Sat next to me on the panel was a female senator and a councillor who were both left-wing politicians. Before the discussion began everyone in the room was shown a documentary. It made for pretty uncomfortable viewing for me, I have to say. Among those interviewed in the documentary was the chief architect of the controversy Jorge Videla. The programme-makers even went to Peru, where they spoke to members of the Peruvian team beaten 6-0 by Argentina in 1978. One of the players, José Velásquez, told how he was performing really well in that match but was taken off shortly after half-time for no obvious reason. On top of that, he added, the substitute introduced in his place was a virtual novice at international level. He was effectively alleging that the Peru coach may have been cooperating with the opposition.

It didn't stop there. The Peruvians also alleged that the Argentine team were drugged, with the validity of that claim only enhanced by a carefully edited quotation from one of our regulars in 1978, Oscar Ortiz. He was shown on the documentary admitting that drugs had always been prevalent in Argentine football, although he did not make a direct reference to the World Cup of 1978. I even saw myself flash up on the screen.

When the film finished the senator put forward an argument that Argentina's World Cup victory of 1978 was corrupt. That it was a victory for Videla. Suddenly all eyes were on me. I was left with the task of defending the legitimacy of my nation's most historic footballing triumph, before a live audience. In response I spoke honestly, from the heart. I told those gathered around me that I never saw any evidence of corruption, and that I'd never taken any sort of drugs at any stage of my career. Questions then came from the floor. "Did you not see anything suspicious at all?" I was asked. "Were you really unaware of what Videla and the junta were doing?" I kept on reiterating that all I had to go on was what I'd seen for myself. Football really was our sole focus at that time.

Sitting on that panel in San Telmo was an uncomfortable experience. It was tough, seeing so many people in front of me who had lost loved ones at the hands of a merciless regime. Tougher still was the fact that I was made to feel in some way responsible for not preventing the suffering. I was really made to sweat. Not that I regret attending the function. It would be easy to 'no comment' every request for an opinion on the subject but I don't wish to do that. I have nothing to hide. The political climate in which we won the World Cup in 1978 remains a real hot potato of a topic. I will always defend the integrity of that triumph, though. Controversial or not, that World Cup success unquestionably lifted the spirits of the Argentine public, as well as the gloomy atmosphere that surrounded them at the time.

After the final itself it seemed as though the entire population had taken to the streets as we left the stadium. The police escorted us away from the ground, with myself, Norberto Alonso and Ossie in the same car. There were thousands of people all around us, cheering and dancing, hugging and crying. It was pandemonium. As soon as the three of us were spotted a wave of bodies descended upon us, launching themselves onto the car and bringing it to a standstill. My apartment was a 15-minute drive from the stadium. That day it took me three hours to get home.

Everyone was basking in the glory of our historic effort. For the first time ever Argentina had claimed football's ultimate prize. I only played a small part in that success – two substitute appearances that amounted to a whole 90 minutes in total. I'll never know if the injury I suffered ahead of the tournament cost me a regular spot in the team. And I'll never be able to feel the same sense of achievement as Fillol, Olguín, Passarella, Galván, Tarantini, Gallego or Kempes, who all started every game. Or Ossie, who only missed one of our seven matches. But I'll always be a World Cup winner. I don't constantly boast of the fact – I leave that to other people, like my friend in Córdoba, Carlos Bruna. Whenever I meet him, in a restaurant or café for example, he announces to all those present, "Look everyone . . . a World Champion." Everyone turns to see who he's talking about and I respond with a coy nod of the head. It's a little bit embarrassing really. Not that I'd ever tell him that. He might stop saying it then.

Chapter Seven
LONDON CALLING

A s phone calls go, it's up there with my more memorable ones. A couple of weeks had passed since our World Cup triumph and Ossie was on the other end of the line. He had a question for me. "Fancy playing in England?"

When you are 25 years old and champion of the world, everything seems like a bit of a breeze. You make a decision and just expect things to work out. I'd never been to England before. I didn't speak the language. And as for the club who were courting us, well, I can't say that I knew a great deal about them either. Actually, I'd never heard of Tottenham Hotspur.

In Argentina, being familiar with English football back then meant being familiar with two teams – Manchester United and Liverpool. That's not because we were ignorant, or insular, but because the extensive global coverage the game currently enjoys, via the Internet, satellite television, and comprehensive newspaper reports, just didn't exist. We were aware of the top, top players like George Best, Bobby Charlton and Bobby Moore, but that was about it really. We never saw English games live on TV.

The focus on European football, for me, lay elsewhere. The

fixtures that set my pulse racing were Inter versus AC Milan, or Real Madrid against Barcelona. When I saw those games listed in the paper it immediately conjured up images of such grand arenas, the famous colours of each club and a whole host of magical players. My ambition was to watch these matches as part of the live audience. While it wasn't an Italian or Spanish team making us an offer, the allure of those countries and their leading clubs made moving to Europe – albeit to England – an enticing proposition.

The whole deal came about, and was completed, incredibly quickly. Because of my limited involvement during the World Cup I returned to Racing immediately after the tournament, while the rest of the victorious squad took a well-earned break. In the Argentine domestic season (which had begun in March) play was suspended throughout June while the World Cup was on, but recommenced one week after the final. I felt fresh and hungry for games so I was involved in the first match back, a 2-1 defeat to Boca Juniors. Normal service was resumed. Until the following weekend, that is. That's when Ossie called. He'd gone home to Córdoba after the World Cup for a rest – he certainly deserved one, after featuring regularly during a campaign of high demands both physically and emotionally. On top of that, he was only able to start the final following a painkilling injection to dull the discomfort caused by a nasty ankle injury.

Of all the conversations myself and Ossie engaged in during the long months preceding the World Cup, moving to England wasn't one of them. We just hadn't considered the prospect. But when Ossie contacted me with news of the proposed deal I was instantly interested. Before I knew it we were sat in a hotel in Buenos Aires alongside the manager of Tottenham

Hotspur, Keith Burkinshaw, and an interpreter. I can't remember the name of the man charged with translating each exchange as negotiations were conducted, but I do know he was the most important person in the room. With two Argentinians who didn't speak English and a Yorkshireman who didn't understand a word of Spanish, someone had to make sense of the situation.

Keith had been glued to the World Cup on TV and was impressed – as many observers had been – with Ossie's skilful presence in the Argentina midfield. I've since become aware that Keith was friends with Harry Haslam, who was manager of Sheffield United at the time. Haslam's network of contacts in the game extended to Argentina, thanks largely to the fact that his assistant, Danny Bergara, was born and raised in Uruguay and had retained strong links throughout South America. In fact, Haslam once travelled over from England with the bold – but genuine – intention of enhancing his Sheffield United squad by snaring a prodigiously talented young player who was fast becoming the talk of Argentinian football. The story goes that the Bramall Lane board baulked at Argentinos Juniors' considerable asking price for a teenager they'd barely heard of, and a deal failed to materialise. With the benefit of hindsight maybe the money men at Sheffield United should have dug a little deeper and taken a chance on the boy Diego Maradona. The Blades subsequently slipped down the divisions while Haslam's number-one target . . . well, we all know what he did next. Haslam didn't leave the country empty-handed though; he did sign an Argentinian player – Alex Sabella – just not the one he had initially set his sights on.

It was Haslam who alerted Keith to the possibility of delving into the Argentinian market. He had been informed that Ossie was available soon after the World Cup, but Sheffield United couldn't afford to sign him. Haslam knew a club that could though. A quick phone call to his old friend Keith and the wheels of the transfer were in motion. Antonio Rattín, the imposing midfielder famously sent off against England at Wembley in 1966, is another who, acting as an intermediary, also played a part in our move. Understandably, Rattín is best remembered in England for his antics in that World Cup quarter-final. Actually, that's probably all he's remembered for in England. Dismissed for dissent – the referee apparently called it "violence of the tongue" – Rattín at first refused to leave the field. The game was held up for several minutes, as the Argentinians protested furiously at the decision. Their captain did eventually leave and play was resumed, albeit with an incensed Rattín supposedly trading insults with spectators as he slowly made his way back to the dressing room. I remember listening to that match on the radio.

After the game Alf Ramsey accused the Argentinians of behaving like animals, and there is a famous image of him physically intervening as one of his players attempts to exchange shirts with an opponent. It all made for a pretty unsavoury episode, which is a real shame. Especially where Rattín is concerned. That display left him with a troublesome reputation, as far as English supporters are concerned, that has lasted to this day. To regard Antonio Rattín as something of a thug is doing him a gross injustice though. In Argentina Rattín is revered among fans of Boca Juniors, the club he served throughout his career. He was a fierce competitor, granted, but he could play as well. With intelligence, a natural understanding of the game and genuine leadership qualities

Rattín was *el Caudillo* – 'the General'. Just ask Boca supporters – they know a player when they see one – or Pelé, who counts Rattín as one of his toughest opponents.

During our negotiations we didn't deal directly with Rattín, but with an Argentinian called Oscar Martínez (Rattín was one of his advisors). He was a businessman, a bit of an entrepreneur I suppose, who was known for organising the prestigious *Torneos de Verano* ('Summer Tournaments') that are held during every pre-season in Argentina. Still contested to this day, the competition was initiated in the late 1960s by Martínez. He had the foresight to host a big football event in the popular beach resort of Mar del Plata, to which thousands of holidaymakers would migrate for the summer. The potential audience for each game was, therefore, huge. Although essentially a series of friendly matches, the *Torneos de Verano* quickly became an important feature of the Argentine football calendar, with all the leading clubs taking part – Boca, River, Independiente and so on – and each game well attended by fans eager to get an early indication of how their team would fare in the new season. Martínez was well connected in the game, and acted as an agent/go-between in our transfer.

Keith, meanwhile, had set off for Argentina with the sole intention of enticing Ossie to White Hart Lane. On paper, many would have considered it something of a futile mission. Ossie had just played a leading role in Argentina's World Cup triumph, while Tottenham had just finished third in the second division behind Bolton Wanderers and Southampton. It was enough to clinch promotion, but only just – goal difference was all that split them and fourth-placed Brighton and Hove Albion.

Because Tottenham were so quick to act no other clubs had been forthcoming with an offer by the time Keith landed in South America. Within minutes of meeting Ossie he'd persuaded him to sign. Just like that. It was an amazing coup. It was only then that I became involved in the transfer. Keith liked the idea of signing a second Argentinian to help ease the process of acclimatising to life in a new country, and Ossie suggested me. Keith contacted Tottenham, they gave him the go-ahead, and negotiations began.

Within half an hour of sitting down with Keith – maybe even less than that – everything had been agreed. Tottenham wanted to sign two World Cup winners, we were excited by the prospect of playing in Europe, and our clubs, Racing and Huracán, were each desperate to bank a substantial transfer fee. Everyone was happy. We asked Keith about the club, and about England, but before long we'd run out of questions. The interpreter looked at myself and Ossie, waiting for us to make some further inquiries. We just shrugged our shoulders. Our minds were made up.

I didn't think twice about making the move. I knew that if I rejected the opportunity I might have to wait a long time before another one came along. Some people thought we were crazy going to a country we knew virtually nothing about. I suppose I just assumed it would work out and signed a three-year contract. It was an adventure, and we went for it.

There was a different agenda when it came to football back then. Nowadays, as soon as a player shows the slightest hint of promise in South America he is whisked off to Europe. Everyone wants to go there, to play for a high-profile club and – more importantly perhaps – land a highly lucrative contract. It hasn't always been like that though. In the 1970s, players didn't dash off to Europe with the same haste. Primarily, I suppose, that's because the incredible riches that are currently on offer in Europe just didn't exist years ago. There wasn't a gaping difference in salaries between clubs on the two continents. As a result there wasn't such an incentive to move abroad, which was reflected in the relatively slow trickle of players who trod that path in those days. Two of Brazil's all-time greats for example, Pelé and Rivelino, never played club football in Europe. It's unimaginable that players of their standing in the modern game would not end up somewhere like Real Madrid, Barcelona, Manchester United or AC Milan. It's destiny if you like. Not so in my time. And if South American players did cross continents it was usually to play in Spain or Italy. Mario Kempes went to Valencia – where he was an unqualified success – while Daniel Bertoni, our other goalscorer in the 1978 World Cup final, headed for Sevilla after the tournament and later spent several seasons in Serie A. Our skipper Daniel Passarella was another who starred in Italy, with Fiorentina and Inter Milan, but not until the 1980s. Keeper Ubaldo Fillol, meanwhile, had a brief spell with Atlético Madrid but, again, not until some time after the 1978 World Cup. Joining a team in Spain or Italy was one thing. Moving to England, on the other hand, was an entirely different concept altogether.

My first impression of Keith Burkinshaw was that he seemed very . . . English. He was honest and frank. A real football man, completely uninterested in the business side of things. The only information he wanted from his chairman, when he phoned from Argentina, was confirmation that Tottenham had the necessary funds in place to complete the double transfer. "Just do it," he was told. Those necessary funds amounted to a total of £700,000. Not a great deal of money in today's market, but back then it was a sizeable fee. To put it into perspective, 12 months earlier – in the summer of 1977 – the two most high-profile transfers involving English clubs had seen Liverpool sell Kevin Keegan to Hamburg for £500,000, and replace him with Celtic's Kenny Dalglish at a cost of £440,000. I'm not sure why, but the £700,000 that Spurs paid for us was not divided equally into each individual transfer. For some reason, I was valued at £375,000 and Ossie at £325,000. Ossie had been one of the World Cup's outstanding performers, whereas I had remained on the fringes. But somewhere along the line my price tag had eclipsed his. People have asked me over the years, "How come you cost more than Ossie?" I tell them it's because I was much bigger than him! There was more of me; Ossie only weighed about 50 kilograms wet through.

In terms of the personal package on offer – and this may come as something of a surprise – the basic wage I accepted at Tottenham was practically the same as I was on at Racing. I can't remember the exact figures, but I may even have taken a slight drop in that respect. However, although the annual salaries at each club were almost identical (roughly £25,000) the overall financial benefits of playing in England were markedly better. Most importantly, you got paid on time in England. At Tottenham, we received our wage every month as promised, without fail. In Argentina, this wasn't the case. There was no such thing as regular payments, and no telling when your money would arrive. If your team were playing particularly badly then you'd be lucky to get paid at all. In addition to that reliability, the signing-on fee involved in transferring clubs provided a significant incentive. With my

15 per cent share I received a lump sum of around £45,000 (once agent's fees and the like had been deducted). That was big money back then, and it enabled me to fulfil a long-standing objective that would have proved difficult to achieve had I stayed at Racing. I bought 300 hectares of farmland in Roque Pérez.

Acquiring my own plot of land represented a major achievement for me. A milestone in my life. Others dream first of buying a big house or a fast car when they come into money. Not me. I wanted that farmland. I can't stress enough just how important that was. Symbolic even. I'd grown up in the open countryside. That was my home, my identity. The anguish I felt as a child every time the landlord came knocking at the door to take our hard-earned money for rent is a feeling that will never leave me. So erasing that unwanted feature from our lives was incredibly satisfying. My father no longer had to pay the rent, and my future was assured.

There were other financial benefits that came with life at our new club. Tottenham paid our electricity bill. They also granted us a monthly allowance for phoning home. All that did was effectively provide me with a little extra cash, because my family didn't have a phone in Roque Pérez. All in all, the switch to England meant we were much better-off financially.

As I've already mentioned, the speed at which the whole deal reached completion was astounding. I think we met Keith on a Tuesday and by the Friday we were on a plane bound for England. We flew to Heathrow, via Madrid, and were picked up at the airport by representatives of our new employers, Tottenham Hotspur Football Club. It was mid-July and it was a beautiful day. "At least I don't have to worry about the weather," I thought. There was my first mistake!

But, although at that point I didn't quite appreciate the rarity of such a sunny occasion, it did make for an encouraging start. There was such a stark contrast between the type of environment we left behind in Argentina and the one we encountered in England. At home the hysterical World Cup celebrations were raging on, as was a violent political conflict. In our new world all seemed calm. From the airport we were taken to a lovely hotel outside London, where we underwent a stringent medical. Electrodes were attached to various parts of our bodies, we had a few scans and X-rays and then sat down while our major joints were pulled around in several different directions. We were both given the all-clear, and Tottenham were free to make a stunning announcement.

Chapter Eight

"HELLO... ME LLAMO RICKY"

Fifteen days after Argentina had been crowned champions of the world two of their triumphant squad sat before a horde of incredulous reporters in a conference room at White Hart Lane. Newly promoted Tottenham Hotspur had just completed one of the greatest transfer swoops of all time, and nobody could quite believe it. "If Spurs had bought Batman and Robin they could scarcely have created more curiosity," wrote one journalist.

I don't know what the assembled media made of it, but for myself and Ossie it was all quite surreal. I'd never experienced a press conference on this scale before. There must have been 60 or 70 people packed into the room. Not only were we World Cup winners joining a club fresh out of the second division – a big enough story in itself – we were regarded as the first genuine overseas players of the post-war era to join an English club. We were pioneers.

Many years ago – at the beginning of the 1930s, so I've been told – the Football Association were opposed to foreign footballers plying their trade in England. So they imposed a two-year residency rule to effectively prevent clubs from shopping abroad. It was a move designed to stop an influx of foreign talent, and remained in place until the European Community ordered a lifting of the "ban" in 1978. That ruling didn't ensure a complete dearth of foreign players in the intervening years though. Some are embedded in FA Cup folklore, thanks to their exploits in the 1950s (what is it about foreign players and FA Cup finals?). The most famous is probably Bert Trautmann, the Manchester City goalkeeper who played the last 15 minutes of the 1956 final with a broken neck. Trautmann was a German soldier captured towards the end of the Second World War. He refused to go back to Germany when the war was over, and instead started a new life in England. After satisfying the residency laws whilst playing amateur football he joined Manchester City. I've also been told the story of the Robledo brothers at Newcastle United, Chile internationals George and Ted. They were born in Chile to a Chilean father, although their English mother raised them in Yorkshire from a young age. Both played in Newcastle's 1952 FA Cup final victory over Arsenal, when George scored the winning goal.

Those examples are few and far between though. Our arrival generated a huge storm of publicity. I've heard people joke that, until we landed at Tottenham, a player in the English league was considered foreign if he came from Scotland, Wales or Ireland. We were big, big news. I must confess to feeling a little startled at that introductory press conference. I wasn't sure what to say. My answers were short and concise, although I do remember the translator giving much longer answers in English than the ones I'd given him in Spanish. I sat there thinking, "I wonder what he's telling them!"

Our feet had hardly touched the ground before we were off again, this time back to Argentina to pick up our families. On the return flight to England I was accompanied by Cristina and her Aunt Rosita. The purpose of Ossie's trip was to visit, rather than collect, his family. His wife Sylvia was heavily pregnant with their second child, Federico, so she stayed in Argentina with their young son Pablo. 'Whirlwind' doesn't come close to describing the state of our existence that summer. Just a few days after landing back in London we took off again, to join up with our new teammates in the Netherlands. Cristina, meanwhile, was left to settle into the house in Chigwell that myself, Cristina, Ossie, Sylvia and their boys would now be calling home. The club sorted out our living arrangements and also provided us with a lady, Judy, to act as a chaperone for Cristina and Rosita. They had a wonderful time visiting the sights of London, wandering around with dictionaries in hand, drinking tea and not understanding a word anyone was saying.

Across Europe in a quiet corner of the Netherlands, Tottenham were preparing for their return to the first division following a one-year stay in the second tier. It was there, in a serene setting close to the Belgian border, that myself and Ossie were introduced to our new colleagues. What I remember most from that first meeting is the difficulty we had in communicating with the players. Nobody in the squad spoke Spanish – why would they? – while the only English word I was familiar with was *hello*. Ossie did at least have a limited grasp of English. But, for me especially, not fully understanding the language proved to be a huge problem during our first few months in England.

We did our best to integrate though. It became evident quite quickly that John Pratt was one of the livelier characters within the group. He joked about the World Cup winners being given special permission to turn up late for pre-season, and sarcastically asked us if we needed a longer rest. But, all this aside, the players made every effort to involve us in all aspects of the training camp. There was a table tennis table where we were staying and, as the best ping-pong player in the team, John picked up a bat and asked if one of us would like to play him. Ossie duly stepped forward. Without revealing that he'd played the game to a high standard back home in Córdoba (we were struggling to reveal anything at all, don't forget) Ossie promptly dealt John a comprehensive beating. Someone else in the squad – I can't remember whom – then challenged me to a game of pool, which I won. "Blimey," said John Pratt (or words to that effect). "These fellas are not just World Cup winners . . . they can do everything!"

Out on the training pitch our initial assessment was that the squad was actually very accomplished. We'd been spoiled, I suppose, training and playing at international level alongside some of the world's elite players like Maradona, Passarella and Kempes. We weren't expecting the same levels of proficiency from our new companions. The technique displayed in those early 'getting-to-know-you' training sessions was highly impressive, though. Ossie and I watched the players go through a series of drills – crossing the ball on the run, finishing with volleys and diving headers – and we thought, "Hang on, most of these players are better than us!"

We were primarily ball dribblers. Our game was based on close control and touch. When it came to striking through the ball there was no telling where it would end up. What I struggled to understand, however, was that too many of the players failed to reproduce their best form when it came to a Saturday afternoon. The technique and composure they showed on the training ground completely eluded them in competitive game situations. I noticed that during games the other boys didn't really want the ball. They would hide, if you like, or panic. It surprised me, because they trained at such a good level. But when it really mattered, it was a different story. There were notable exceptions though. Glenn Hoddle stood out immediately, whether it be on the practice pitch or on a match day. From the very first time I saw him play it was obvious that he had a special talent. Steve Perryman was another who caught the eye. 'Stevie P' was the best professional I've ever seen. Technically excellent, his performance levels never dropped below seven and a half out of ten in matches or in training. He worked extremely hard and always set the right example. He was the perfect captain.

Everyone at Spurs did their best to make us feel welcome. Don McAllister was a really nice guy; he was very patient with me. Terry Naylor was the funniest of all the players. Terry loved to sing. He even recorded a few songs, and when I saw him recently in London he gave me a copy of his CD. "What a nice gift," I thought. It was torture! Don't tell him I said that. I'd rather listen to Ossie sing! Don't tell *him* I said that. As for another of our fullbacks, the Scotsman John Gorman, I definitely had no chance of understanding a word he was saying. Ossie and I did use to pick up the gist of certain conversations. Sometimes we would be sat in the changing room at training or before a match and someone – usually John Pratt – would make a comment that everyone else would start laughing at. We would look at each other and say, "I think that was at our expense."

Of an evening, Ossie and I would reflect on the events of each day. "Oh dear," we would say. "Nothing is similar to Argentina – the training, the style of play. This is not what we're used to." We knew nothing about England or English football. Every morning I would wake up and think, "I wonder what will happen today." Every day, everything was brand new.

Chapter Nine
LOST

Carlos Tévez featured in a documentary I watched on TV not so long ago. The programme gave an insight into how well *Carlitos* had taken to life in England. Like myself, he initially left South America (where he was playing for Corinthians of Brazil) to join a London club (West Ham United). After playing a major role in West Ham's unlikely escape from relegation in 2007, he was lured up north by Manchester United manager Alex Ferguson. Two years and two Premier League titles later he changed clubs again, as United's reluctance to turn his long-term loan arrangement into a permanent deal saw rivals Manchester City take the Argentine striker across town.

I couldn't help but make a connection between Carlos's situation and the predicament I had found myself in some 30 years earlier. The parallels – an Argentine footballer moving to England amidst a blaze of publicity – were obvious. That's just about where the comparisons end, though. Living in a foreign land 7,000 miles from home is an entirely different experience nowadays than it was in 1978. I can vouch for that. If it hadn't been for the fact that Ossie was alongside me at Tottenham, I would have gone back to Argentina at the end of my first season in England and not returned. I am sure of that. I will for ever cherish my time at Spurs, because – over the years – I grew to love the place. Tottenham will always be my team. To begin with though, I felt so isolated. It was an unbelievably difficult time.

Due to major advancements in the field of telecommunication it's now so simple to maintain contact with friends and family from any corner of the globe. In 1978, don't forget, that wasn't so. There was no internet to occupy our time or to keep abreast of events back home, no webcams and no mobile phones. Texting and e-mail were foreign words in any language. There were no satellite TV channels, so we had to make do with the three that were on offer – BBC1, BBC2 and ITV. All in English, of course, and all incomprehensible for us confused Argentinians. There were some television programmes that were viewable despite the language barrier. *Match of the Day* quickly became my favourite, followed by wildlife documentaries. Not only did I find the content of these shows interesting, it didn't matter that I couldn't understand the commentary. I could follow the programmes visually because the pictures told the story. I was lost, however, when anything else came on.

In terms of maintaining contact with loved ones back home, that was particularly hard. It was difficult to speak with my family because, thousands of miles away in Roque Pérez, they did not have a telephone in the house. Instead I wrote letters to my father. Instant messaging this was not; I would receive a reply about 15 days later. We did occasionally speak, but that required my father to travel 15 kilometres into town to use a telephone. Even then we had to arrange a specific time to talk, so that I could make sure I was in, and sometimes he had to wait as long as three hours for a connection to London. What a challenge. Carlos, meanwhile, has no such problems. When he gets bored or lonely, he revealed on the documentary, he pays for a group of friends to fly over from Argentina and stay with him. Good luck to him. He's a fine player and I certainly don't begrudge him his wealth. But we couldn't afford to do that. It was definitely harder to settle in our time.

It's not like we were completely naive though. We knew it would be tough at the start. Whilst I was away in the Netherlands during my first pre-season as a Tottenham player I spoke to Cristina every day. She told me how much she missed Argentina. Tottenham, for their part, were brilliant. They took great care of us, getting us into a house and laying everything on for us, making sure the fridge was always full. To begin with we all lived in the same four-bedroom house in Chigwell, with myself, Cristina and Ossie joined by Sylvia and the Ardiles boys Pablo and Federico soon after Federico was born in the September of 1978. It was like one big family. That was until we bought our own houses, next door to each other in Turnford, which were conveniently located close to the club's Cheshunt training ground.

Integrating into society was hard. I couldn't understand anyone, either in person or on TV or the radio. I couldn't read the newspapers. Every month or two I went to the Argentine embassy in London just to converse with people in my native language. I had encountered such problems attempting to communicate with English people that – weirdly – I experienced some sort of paranoia. It got to a stage where I began to wonder if anyone could understand me at all. I almost forgot what it felt like to hold a normal conversation outside of my own home. Such was my state of anguish, trauma almost, that I feared they wouldn't even make sense of what I was saying when I visited my compatriots at the embassy.

Ossie and I were invited to a number of official receptions and functions when we first went to England. We felt it was our duty to attend, on behalf of the club, but if I'm honest those events were pretty torturous affairs. People were forever standing up and making speeches. We had no idea what was being said, and we didn't get any of the jokes. Imagine being sat next to someone for two hours without saying a word. It was an uncomfortable, dejecting experience. Failing to interact with people was particularly depressing for me. I've always been a sociable type. I love to talk. I need that contact with people. Ossie is a different character, although he understood more than me.

I began to think about religion even though it was a subject I'd never taken an interest in at home. I started to go to church in search of something that would help me feel a sense of community. I found a Spanish priest nearby, in Loughton, and visited him every week for about six months or so. At no stage did I develop any strong religious beliefs. He was someone I could talk to more than anything else. I just longed to feel settled.

We had English lessons twice a week. It was all very rudimentary. Our teacher was an Englishman named Matthew who – and this seems odd now – wasn't a fluent Spanish-speaker. Matthew would come to our house, where Ossie, Cristina, Sylvia and I would sit around a table while Matthew picked up a variety of objects and informed us of the English term for each one. "Spoon," he would state, whilst holding the item aloft, "glass" and so on. Matthew was a lovely man with incredible patience; I really can't praise him enough. He passed away some time ago but we still receive a Christmas card each year from his wife. The problem was, after a year of lessons with Matthew his Spanish had improved far more than my English had. For someone like myself, who did not have a secondary education, understanding the grammar of a new language and constructing sentences presented such a daunting challenge. After a while I could work out what reporters were asking me, but I was unable to articulate an appropriate answer. It was so frustrating; I felt so stupid.

We were so reliant on other people, which was a strange concept for me. Since an early age I'd been used to helping myself to stuff. As a kid, if we needed milk I would go and milk the cows. If we needed potatoes I would go and fetch some. In England that independence was compromised. Having said that, we appreciated all the help we were afforded from people like Eddie Buckley, who was effectively our first agent at Tottenham. We endorsed various products through Eddie. My first set of golf clubs, for example, was obtained in this manner. Eddie made a call, Ossie and I were pictured with some clubs and then they were handed to us for keeps. There was a parallel business emerging alongside football and Eddie helped us deal with that side of things. He did more than that though. Eddie became a really good friend.

Driving in England was another challenge that took me a while to get to grips with.. More specifically, driving on the left side of the road – and not the right, as we do in Argentina – posed an awkward challenge. I often clipped the curb when turning left, and sometimes turned the wrong way altogether. The glare of headlights coming straight towards me always served as a handy reminder that I'd messed up again. People take more care behind the wheel in England. In Argentina we don't respect other drivers. The wide roads of Buenos Aires sometimes resemble a race track, with all the cars competing against each other. Keith Burkinshaw once asked me what the speed limit is in Argentina and I said "I don't know." The other players at Spurs would say to me, "Ricky, why are you driving so fast? Has your wife told you to rush home?" I didn't even realise I was driving fast.

Besides the issues of (possibly) speeding and working out which side of the road I was supposed to be on there was another fundamental problem that stumped both myself and Ossie when we first started driving in England. We had no idea where we were going. We got lost every day. Every five minutes actually. Asking for directions wasn't really an option; Ossie's grasp of English was poor and mine was virtually non-existent. It was impossible for us to get anywhere. Where was satnav when we needed it?

The one time we did ask for help, soon after we'd arrived in London, we ended up wishing we hadn't. We agreed to meet an Argentinian friend in the city and decided that Harrods would be a convenient meeting place, seeing as it was a famous landmark that we were all vaguely familiar with. How difficult could it be to find one of the world's biggest department stores? Too difficult, it turned out, for a couple of aimlessly hopeful foreigners with little knowledge of the city's streets and even less sense of direction. We did not lack ambition though. "We'll find it eventually," we reckoned. We didn't find it, of course; we never found our way anywhere. As time passed we became increasingly desperate. Finally we approached a policeman and, in pigeon English, asked him where Harrods was. "I'll show you," he said. "Just follow me." Proud of our successful attempt to communicate with the locals we got back in our car and followed the policeman. What a relief. That policeman was our saviour, we figured. Or he would have been, had he not misunderstood our initial inquiry. He took us all the way to Harrow.

An easy mistake to make, I suppose: Harrods, Harrow. We followed that police car for miles. Even we knew something wasn't quite right, as we made our way out of the city. So much for asking for directions. It didn't take us long to work out that the most sensible thing to do when travelling around London was to take the underground.

Despite our limited familiarity with the local area Cristina and I did enjoy exploring our new surroundings. We used to jump in the car and drive around for a while, admiring the architecture of the old houses and buildings. I loved the sense of history. I've never been one for sitting inside my house for long periods – when I was a child I only went indoors to sleep. In England, though, we were not so familiar with the area, and therefore a bit more restricted in what we could do. We rarely went to restaurants. (Ossie, in contrast, has always loved going to restaurants.) When I was at Quilmes, in the early 1970s, I shared a house with several other players, and we all ate together. In Tucumán I was in a hotel for a while, and once again I would eat in front of a crowd every day. In England, I was happy to have dinner at home.

On the subject of food and drink, this was another interesting topic for us. Mealtime at the training ground was an enlightening experience. We'd be served up roast beef and a selection of vegetables that looked as though they'd been cooked for days. And why did everyone eat baked beans all the time? Baked beans for breakfast, baked beans for lunch. We didn't even know what baked beans were. And as for fish and chips! I wasn't a huge fan. I tried to avoid fried food in order to keep my weight down.

Drinking was another story altogether. I'm not teetotal but I don't think I've ever been drunk. In Argentina it was normal to have one or two cold bottles of beers in the summer or maybe a couple of whiskies if you were out in a bar. There wasn't a big drinking culture, especially not among professional footballers. As a player, consuming alcohol in front of others was not really accepted. In England it was encouraged! I remember the first time we visited a pub in England. The players were ordering pints of beer. I couldn't believe it. A whole pint? Are they going to drink all of that? I wondered. How naive I was. "You must drink at least one before you leave," we were ordered. This was all a big surprise to me. Sometimes the players would drink beer – warm beer – on the coach back from away games. Ossie and I compromised by drinking wine instead, which wasn't really the done thing. That was more the directors' preferred tipple.

Although our new teammates did their utmost to make us feel part of things I often said no to offers of a night out (unless the venue was La Caverna in Enfield, a restaurant owned by my good friend Luis Gallego). I would make excuses, putting up stupid barriers to avoid placing myself in awkward situations. It all came down to the fact that I couldn't converse in English. It made me feel foolish. It was my own fault of course. I didn't make as much effort as I should have done to learn the language. Instead of embracing the subject I pushed it to one side. I suppose that in the back of my mind I always saw my stay in England as being a temporary one. I reasoned that before long I would go home, so why devote time to learning a language that I would only need for a brief period? It was the wrong attitude and one that stifled my natural personality. I'm extremely sociable and talkative in my native tongue, but in England I must have seemed quiet and reserved. I just couldn't be myself.

Chapter Ten

FOOTBALL... BUT NOT AS WE KNEW IT

W hile the process of finding our feet in a foreign land continued to present us with a seemingly never-ending series of hurdles to negotiate, the real business for Ossie and I began at the City Ground, Nottingham, on 19th August 1978.

Pre-season that year was absolute chaos. People seemed to gather wherever we went, in their hundreds at training and in their thousands at friendly matches. Our every move was scrutinised. We were in the newspapers every single day. "Ricky did this in training" or "Ossie did that". The media were fascinated with us. As a result, we were recognised wherever we went. It was impossible not to recognise us, I suppose, because we went everywhere together. Even now, if I'm out in England on my own people often take no notice of me. But if I'm with Ossie then they immediately say, "Oh look, there's Ossie and Ricky". Everyone was curious, with the unprecedented arrival of two World Cup-winning foreign footballers sparking a huge wave of intrigue. All eyes were on

Tottenham's pioneering South American duo, and the situation had reached fever pitch.

We were presented with the most testing of contests in which to officially begin our stint as Tottenham Hotspur players. Nottingham Forest away. Brian Clough's side had won the championship in the previous season, and would go on to win the next two European Cups. For a newly-promoted outfit in the process of incorporating a couple of untried imports into their team, it was not the kindest of opening-day fixtures.

England in the spring and summer is a beautiful place. I realised that as soon as I arrived. The sun was shining and all the pitches were in immaculate condition, with a complete covering of lush green grass. The City Ground surface was one such example. Forty-one thousand, two hundred and twenty-three people – including a huge mass of Spurs fans – were crammed inside the City Ground that day. Just how many more were locked outside is anyone's guess, but I've been told that thousands were unable to get in. It was mayhem. To give you some idea of the interest that our presence generated, the average league attendance at Nottingham Forest in that 1978/79 season was 29,500 – some 12,000 down on the crowd that witnessed our first division debut. Only the visit of Liverpool drew more spectators to the City Ground that season.

There was no translator with us, so I sat next to Ossie in the dressing room beforehand and listened to our pre-match brief without understanding a single word of it. During those first few months I would say to Ossie, "Don't go anywhere. I'll have nobody to talk to." Keith Burkinshaw indicated on a board how the team would line up – Daines, Perryman,

McAllister, Lacy, Gorman, Taylor, Ardiles, Hoddle, Villa, Armstrong and Moores. By gesturing towards specific areas on the board Keith highlighted the positions in which he wanted myself and Ossie to operate. That was it as far as our instructions went. Keith then handed over to his assistant Pat Welton. Once again, I didn't have a clue what was being said. Pat was very aggressive though, and with every second word he slammed his fist into the palm of his other hand. Ossie and I looked at each other and wondered what on earth was going on. What exactly was he asking us to do? Punch our opponents? Surely not. We soon realised that it was just Pat's way of motivating the team.

It was an extraordinary experience. Everything was new and I couldn't really take in what was happening. We'd played in a few friendlies but there had been a constant stream of substitutions in those games. We still weren't familiar with the team's style, how they functioned or how best we could fit into the system. I was a little anxious as the game was about to start, but once it got underway those nerves soon disappeared. During the match, in every single minute something different happened. As reigning champions Forest were expected to begin the defence of their title with a victory, so when Martin O'Neill scored for the home side, collecting two points – the reward for winning a league encounter in those days – seemed a formality.

Forest had to settle for just the one point, though, because I scored an equaliser. The ball was played across the edge of the six-yard box – by Peter Taylor, I think – and I feinted to shoot. As I did so Peter Shilton bought the dummy and flung himself to one side. I shifted the ball onto my other foot and tapped the ball in. I'd scored on debut – past an England international goalkeeper – away from home against the best team in the country, to earn my team an unexpected point. I said to Ossie after the game "English football is easy!" It was a joke of course; the games that followed, however, provided us with nothing to laugh about at all.

Four days after that encouraging start to the season in Nottingham we made our home debuts. On a Wednesday night under the lights at White Hart Lane, almost 48,000 turned up to catch a glimpse of the new-look Spurs. And what a welcome they gave us. We received a rapturous reception, with supporters recreating scenes from the World Cup in Argentina by throwing ticker tape into the air as we emerged from the dressing room. As for our opponents that night, they were the source of some confusion to me. Aston Villa? When I saw the name I wondered if it was some kind of reference to me. Like most English clubs, they were unknown where I came from. I soon discovered that Aston Villa was indeed a football team though, and an extremely good one at that. They put a real dampener on the evening by winning easily, 4-1. They were completely superior to us. Villa were a tight, compact unit, whereas we played – badly, it must be said – like a group of individuals that had been hastily cobbled together. I, for one, struggled to get into the game. Glenn Hoddle's penalty proved to be nothing more than a consolation on a disappointing, anticlimactic night for us.

Any lingering hopes that the Villa setback had been a one-off, and that perhaps our team wasn't as frail as that performance had suggested, were well and truly dismissed at Anfield ten days later. We lost 7-0. I wanted to break records with Tottenham, but not like this – it was the club's heaviest ever defeat. Liverpool were the perfect team. They moved the ball so quickly, making two or three passes in rapid succession and then having three or four players charge into the box whenever they attacked. In Kenny Dalglish they had the best player I faced during my spell in England. Dalglish possessed great control, he used his body so well, and in front of goal he never seemed to miss. Ray Kennedy and Graeme Souness were fantastic midfielders, and so too was Terry McDermott. He was an outstanding player and a touch underrated perhaps. He wasn't a talker, just an excellent footballer, constantly passing and moving. Liverpool were *the* team throughout my time in England.

Personally, and from the team's point of view, that thrashing at Anfield was a crushing experience. We were awful, and Liverpool were so much better than us. I don't remember losing any other game 7-0 in my life. It was embarrassing, and the dressing room was silent after the game. About 20 years later, incidentally, Phil Neal and Alan Kennedy – who were both in the Liverpool side that day – visited my home town in Argentina, Roque Pérez, to play for a touring Hong Kong XI in a game that I was asked to arrange. It was a great event. We had a big barbeque, and our visitors drank Roque Pérez dry on a raucous night of singing and dancing. Best of all, Roque Pérez, with me in the team, won the match 7-0. I said to the Liverpool boys afterwards, "Finally – revenge!"

Rewind 20 years, mind you, and our plight was no laughing matter. For a start, football was a completely different game in England to the one I knew in Argentina. Unbelievably so, in fact. In England at that time the general approach was quick, simple and direct. Defenders would hit long balls into the channels and midfielders were urged to get forward in support. From there, crosses would be fired into the box, where a bunch of players would fight to get on the end of it. I couldn't quite get used to it. To begin with, I was dropping deep to receive the ball – that was a natural movement for me – only to see it launched deep into the opposing half of the pitch. I would then run upfield to get nearer the ball, but more often than not it would be sent sailing back over my head. I could sort of understand why we played in that manner, because we had big strikers like Gerry Armstrong who could win headers and hold the ball up when necessary. We played to our strengths in that respect. But I seemed to be running constantly without getting anywhere near the ball. I just couldn't get into a position where I was of any use to the team. On top of that I lost my competitive edge when I first came to England. I didn't know my teammates and I wasn't familiar with the opposition. I was surrounded by strangers, which for some reason seemed to dilute my competitive spirit.

After that trouncing at Anfield we suffered another shock, as Third Division Swansea City came to White Hart Lane and knocked us out of the League Cup. That 3-1 defeat – a game in which I scored our only goal – dealt the side's confidence a huge blow. The season was barely into September and we were already approaching crisis point. Somehow we found a way out of our slump though, recording narrow back-to-back victories over Bristol City and Leeds United to ease the tension. We also won consecutive games at the beginning of October, but I can't claim to have played a part in either of those successes; by that time I was out of the team. My struggle to embrace the dynamic nature of English football saw me taken out of the side, and I spent much of the time leading up to Christmas on the bench. At a time when I was finding it equally hard to settle off the pitch, losing my place in the line-up just magnified my troubles. I felt completely detached. I wasn't happy on the pitch and I wasn't happy off it. I'd never imagined it would be that difficult. It was a tough, tough time.

As the season wore on, the condition of the pitches began to influence proceedings. You rarely see a bad pitch in the Premier League now, but in the 1970s and 1980s the playing surfaces during the winter months were so muddy. One of the worst was Old Trafford – you didn't want to be playing Manchester United away from home in December or January. I liked to run with the ball at my feet, but dribbling across a heavy, sticky surface was difficult for anyone.

Nothing could have prepared us for that first winter abroad. Every day we learned something new in England, and the weather was a constant source of bemusement. "What is it going to do today?" we would wonder. I'll never forget the morning I got out of bed and drew the curtains back only to find that everything in view had turned white. "Cristina!" I shouted. "Snow!" We'd never seen any before. The scene outside our house was like a picture postcard, complete with snow-lined pine trees. It was beautiful. The winter of 1978/79 was very severe, but to us it was all part of the adventure. Quite exciting even.

The first time it snowed, Ossie and I just assumed we would be given the day off. Surely it wasn't possible to train in this weather, we thought (and hoped, I must admit). No such luck. We made our way along the snowy roads to the training ground where, sure enough, it was business as usual. The pitch wasn't frozen, after all. As soon as I entered the changing room I realised my uncertainty regarding the conditions wasn't shared by the rest of the playing squad. They couldn't wait to get out there! It was like watching a bunch of excited schoolboys. When I came off the training field that day – having taken one or two unexpected snowballs to the head – I experienced a completely new sensation. My feet had gone to sleep. They were frozen stiff. I had to massage them to get the blood circulating again. And as for the team bath, that was way too hot to get in. I stood by the side dipping my toe in the water while my colleagues dived in without a care. We Argentinians are a bit more precious than the British in such situations.

Actually, I grew to love training in the snow. The ball ran truer than it did on an uneven muddy surface, and the snow always cushioned your fall (which was handy if you were up against the likes of Graham Roberts and Paul Miller!). The attitude of the Tottenham players was brilliant. They just got on and trained, regardless of the weather or that day's specific programme. In Argentina, if a squad of 25 players turn up for training, you can guarantee that at least five or six will complain of feeling tired, and won't want to exert themselves. In England nobody made excuses; they just went ahead and did what was asked of them.

That general approach to training was different from what I'd been used to. It was so intense. This presented me with a real shock. In Argentina, the type of player that I was – a number 10 – is treated differently. *Pampered* is probably an appropriate term. If you didn't feel quite right and wanted to skip training then the manager would say, "No problem". In England, you'd have to think again. Argentinian managers may take their number 10 to one side and have a quiet word if the team is not scoring enough goals, or creating enough chances, because that is largely the responsibility of a *número diez*. But otherwise, they're left to function at their own pace. I brought some bad habits with me to England, and training was one area in which I found it hard to adapt. It's not easy to change your mentality when you're 25 or 26 years of age. Every Monday morning we would be back on the practice pitch working at full tilt. I would think to myself, "This is a bit much. I only played on Saturday." I'd become accustomed to taking it easy in the early part of the week. It was a completely different approach.

Football, in my opinion, is not all about running. The word we use in Argentina to best describe my role as a player is *enganche*, which translates to 'hook'. It refers to those who play 'free' behind the attackers, acting as a link – or hook – between the midfield and the forward line. It's a position that does not require high energy levels and intensity. I never used to tear about all over the pitch. Plenty of players did, especially in England, and I admired them for that. But it just wasn't in my nature. I always joke that whoever leads the running in training must be the worst player – it's God's way of compensating for a lack of talent! I loved the ball. I was used to having it at my feet, and in Argentina I was the player that my teammates would look to supply when they had possession. If I had to compare myself to a player in the modern game it would be Juan Román Riquelme, who returned to Boca following a spell in Europe with Barcelona and Villarreal. Riquelme is highly technical. He doesn't go hunting for the ball, his colleagues feed him. From there he can dictate proceedings.

So I wasn't the most physical of trainers. Ossie, on the other hand, was able to adjust straight away. He was extremely fit, a much better runner than I was. The extended warm-ups, the jumping and sprinting, the weights – I found all that a bit boring. Having said that, we did see plenty of the ball in training as well. Probably more so than in Argentina, which may come as a surprise.

I only understood what being a true professional meant when I came to England. The attitude of the players was top, top class. Those who were not the most naturally talented would arrive at training early and give their all, even if their chances of getting into the team were minimal. I really liked that. When those same players were left out of the side they still rooted for the team, which was another thing that impressed me. In Argentina, a dropped player, or one that didn't figure prominently in the manager's plans, would put on a *mala cara* ('bad face') and perhaps hope that the team would struggle in his absence.

While my efforts to adjust to a different tempo on the training field continued Keith set about identifying the position in which I would be most productive when it really mattered, come three o'clock on a Saturday afternoon. Keith spoke to me, and to Ossie, at great length, in an attempt to integrate us into the team. Keith was always striving to find a way of making me feel more comfortable on the pitch. Deciding exactly where I best fitted into the team was a problem that took several months, maybe a year even, to resolve. I started out on the left wing. Peter Taylor – a natural winger – was on the opposite side, with Glenn and Ossie in the middle. But I was never a left winger. I wasn't conditioned to spend the entire game motoring up and down the flank. Tony Galvin was, though, and he soon came along to relieve me of my left-sided duties. I was next deployed at centre forward. Keith assessed my attributes – height, strength, good control, a powerful shot in both feet – and thought I might be suited to a more advanced position, as a focal point of the attack. That didn't really work either. I had my back to goal and a defender right up against me, as passes were fizzed in at chest level or in the air. I was never a good header the ball, so it was time for Keith to shuffle things around again. Eventually, I was afforded a free role behind the strikers, which was a position that didn't really exist in England at that time.

With or without me in the team Spurs' form fluctuated throughout the 1978/79 campaign, but we managed to remain around the mid-table region for virtually all of it. A spectacular blip came around Christmas time when a Liam Brady-inspired Arsenal won 5-0 at White Hart Lane. I didn't play in that match but I did regain my place soon after and started regularly from there on in.

While I took my time to settle in at Tottenham, Ossie adapted to our change of environment very quickly. Off the pitch his superior understanding of the English language saw him act as my interpreter, while on the pitch he found it a lot easier than me to claim possession of the ball. What he also did was take on all-comers from the first moment we arrived. You name it – referees, linesmen, opponents – Ossie was ready to fight them all! Referees were more lenient in England. They preferred to defuse confrontations by talking to players, rather than brandishing yellow cards at the first hint of a dispute. "Next time you'll go into the book," they would say. That leniency didn't wash with Ossie though. He still berated them at every opportunity. And as for physical altercations with opposing players, he was forever launching himself into them. Because he was so quick and nimble he usually got to the ball first, after which his speed and excellent close control made it difficult for anyone to relieve him of possession. Frustrated opponents often resorted to kicking him, and Ossie would react. He was a feisty competitor. To help protect him, I would put myself in between Ossie and whoever he was angry with at the time. I used to wind him up by saying, "Why are you fighting these guys when you've got such a puny body?!" There was nothing of him, he was so small and lean.

These clashes were not uncommon, I have to say. Ossie and I didn't receive the most pleasant of receptions from opponents during our early games as Tottenham players. Inevitably, our arrival sparked a certain degree of hostility among some of the players we came up against. I've no doubt a few of them probably set out to intimidate us. Maybe they didn't agree with foreign players coming to play in English football. Maybe it was a question of pride. Or maybe they just felt that we were a bit fragile, and that an aggressive approach would scare us out of games. This wasn't the case, of course. I didn't understand exactly what it was our opponents were saying, even though I quickly became familiar with one or two words that always seemed to pepper their verbal threats. Most of them began with F. But you didn't need to be fluent in English to recognise the intentions of these players. The tone of their voices, or the expression on their faces saw to that. I knew they weren't politely asking me how well I was finding life in my new surroundings, or wishing me the very best of luck in my new venture. It didn't bother me though. I just took no notice. If a player is intimidated by that kind of practice then they don't get to play at the highest level. Besides, in Argentina the verbal abuse was much worse. There the players would go to great lengths to unsettle opponents, finding out beforehand about a player and his family, looking for any events or incidents in his private life that may be the cause of some shame or anguish. Anything that could be used to taunt and upset that player during a match.

Of all the various difficulties that I encountered on and off the pitch I can honestly say that I don't think the significant weight of pressure that may be expected to accompany such a high-profile transfer was one of them. When I joined Racing Club of Buenos Aires from Atlético Tucumán in 1977 the fee was a new record in Argentina. I was thrust into the spotlight, and felt under pressure to produce something special in every single game. The expectations were huge, and I believe this had a debilitating effect on my form. At Tottenham, that wasn't so. I was unaware of the press coverage I was getting because I couldn't read the reports, and I didn't understand the TV pundits when they were expressing their opinions. I had no idea if they were being especially critical or not. As a result, it was impossible to gauge precisely what the expectations were – whether or not the general consensus was that I should be trying harder, or playing better, or even dropped – or just how closely my performances were being monitored and assessed. I knew that I wasn't performing at my very best, but I suppose I was living in a type of cocoon. Ignorance was bliss. Grasping the English language was the most challenging aspect of moving to Tottenham, but in one respect at least, my lack of understanding probably did me a favour.

It wasn't just the language that puzzled me. English football was full of customs that I hadn't encountered in Argentina. Like the Players' Lounge, for example. We all went straight home after a game in Argentina, especially if we'd lost. The only people who wanted to see you after a defeat in Argentina were your family. At Tottenham – win, lose or draw – the players congregated in the bar for a post-match drink. It helped to foster team spirit. What I found really strange was that players from both teams would gather in the same room. The concept of spending 90 minutes in fierce competition with an opposing player and then standing beside him – smartly dressed in shirt and tie, drinking beer – was a new one for me. Sometimes a player would come up to me and say, "Sorry I kicked you today, Ricky. Fancy a drink?" I loved this tradition!

I discovered this was typical of the sportsmanship that existed within English football. Out on the pitch, from the first whistle to the last, a player would fight hard to defend his team and his reputation. Defenders relished the prospect of engaging in physical battles or, as I mentioned earlier, verbal intimidation. As a player who continually attempted to take on opponents I'm sure I must have ended up on the rough end of some overzealous challenges, but I don't remember there ever being any malicious intent. Mixing with our adversaries after the contest allowed me to see another side to these players. With their aggressive 'match' demeanour removed, I could see that these people were decent guys.

Tottenham took maximum points from the last two games to finish 11th in 1979. It was a decent end to a testing season for the team and for me in particular, as I scored in both of those victories against Bolton Wanderers and West Bromwich Albion. Considering it was the club's first season back amongst the elite, 11th place represented something of an achievement. In the following season we accrued a similar number of points but ended up in 14th place. Again we made a poor start that season and again we recovered to spend the bulk of it in mid-table territory, with our most notable wins coming against Nottingham Forest and Liverpool. I was a regular starter in that 1979/80 campaign before missing the last two months due to a serious injury sustained in an FA Cup tie against Liverpool at White Hart Lane. It was an injury so severe, in fact, that not only did it threaten to end my overseas adventure after just a couple of seasons in England, but also my professional career altogether.

The identity of the opponent whose challenge caused the damage was Graeme Souness, but don't go jumping to conclusions. It wasn't a foul. Despite his fearsome reputation, I would never regard Souness as simply a hard man. That would be doing him a gross injustice. Far from being just a midfield enforcer, he was a wonderful footballer. On this occasion, we both went for the ball – a 50-50 challenge – and I managed to get there first. But just as I tried to twist away from him he slid in, making firm contact with the ball. My knee, positioned at an awkward angle, took the force of the impact and something went. I didn't fall down; when I attempted to put weight on my foot, though, I knew immediately that something wasn't right. My leg felt like jelly. I was examined the next day and informed that I'd torn the lateral ligament in my knee. My season was over. I had an operation immediately, after which my leg was set in a cast for six weeks from ankle to thigh.

Tearing knee ligaments is a fairly common injury in football. Nowadays it's a problem that, thanks to advancements in the medical field, can be fixed straight away with little fuss. With well-developed rehabilitation programmes also in place, affected players often return just as strong – if not stronger – than they were before sustaining the injury. It wasn't as simple as that in 1980, though. The staff at Tottenham were genuinely concerned. They informed me that the injury was bad. Really bad. They feared the worst, and couldn't guarantee that I'd make a full recovery. Then came a suggestion that hit me like a bolt of lightning. I should take an insurance pay-out, they said, and retire from professional football.

I was 27 years old. I was in the process of starting a family. I'd spent my whole youth aspiring to be a footballer and my whole senior life being a footballer. I didn't know much else. I didn't want to do much else. I had a big decision to make. Or did I? I may have struggled to settle in England but I wasn't ready to give up and pack the game in altogether. I was a *futbolista*. Besides, Tottenham had yet to see the best of me. There was plenty more to come. In the end there was no decision to make. I dismissed the suggestion of retirement straight away.

Despite suffering the turmoil of a long-term career-threatening injury I was fortunate enough to have other, more positive, things on my mind at that time, namely the birth of our first child. María Eugenia ('Maru') was born on 21st April 1980 at Chase Farm Hospital in Enfield. She was nearly born *on the way* to the hospital though, thanks to Ossie. Let me explain. I was unable to drive because my leg was in plaster, so when Cristina's contractions – which had started in the early hours of the morning – reached a point where we had to get her to the hospital that evening, my reliable friend Ossie volunteered to take the wheel. Not content with simply driving us there, Ossie felt inclined to help further. "I know a shortcut," he said confidently. And then got lost. I have to say, Ossie knew his way around a football pitch like no one else. On the roads, though, he had no idea where he was going. With Cristina getting increasingly tired and anxious in the front, me stretched out across the back seat with my leg in plaster and Ossie driving round in circles, it took us ages to find the hospital. Eventually we did find it, and just minutes after arriving our beautiful daughter was born.

Not long after Maru came along I began a recovery process that I hoped would get me fit again for the start of the new season. The rehabilitation procedure that I underwent provides another example of just how far the game has evolved since my days as a player. Tottenham decided not to leave me under the supervision of the club's physio Mike Varney. They suspected I might say, "Come on Mike, let's finish early today", and that I would maybe look for shortcuts. (They knew me too well!) Instead, I was sent to a hospital some 50 miles away. I drove there every day for six weeks, arriving promptly for a nine o'clock start and finishing at four. I was joined by 40 or 50 other people, from all walks of life, who were also recovering from injury.

What was instantly evident was that most of those in attendance were far worse off than me. Some of them had been involved in car or motorbike accidents, for example. I was inspired by the courage demonstrated by those men and women, some of whom had been severely hurt. It was a humbling experience. In comparison, there was barely anything wrong with me at all. We had a physical trainer who gave the whole class a general warm-up to music – my lack of rhythm meant that I struggled to master most routines – before we split into smaller groups. After about one week I could walk around, so I began making tea and handing out biscuits to those whose injuries had left them incapable of helping themselves. I tried to assist the staff wherever I could. It wasn't much of a contribution, but it was more than I was able to offer on the pitch. Until the following season, that is.

Chapter Eleven
CONTENDERS AT LAST

I would like to go on record as saying that Garth Crooks was an excellent striker.

Signed from Stoke City in the summer of 1980, he arrived at White Hart Lane as part of Keith Burkinshaw's ongoing attempts to revive the fortunes of Tottenham Hotspur. That process had begun in earnest following the club's promotion in 1978, when Ossie and I were joined in our new surroundings by John Lacy, a central defender lured across London from Fulham. The following year saw Terry Yorath added to the squad, with the former Leeds United man providing a welcome dose of experience in a side that was beginning to feature a promising crop of youth-team products such as Chris Hughton, Paul Miller, Micky Hazard and Mark Falco. Signs of a revival had been evident but, as the manager needed no reminding, they were all too sparing.

After two seasons back in the top-flight – both of which had finished with his side occupying mid-table positions of 11th and 14th – Keith was determined to build on the promising foundations at his disposal and develop a stylish team capable of mounting a serious challenge for honours. The acquisition of Garth, for £600,000, proved to be a highly astute piece of business. Another forward, Steve Archibald, was also signed that summer, and the two formed a deadly alliance almost immediately. Their goals were a crucial feature of the success that Tottenham enjoyed in the first half of the 1980s, and Garth was most definitely an integral part of the team. A prolific striker, he possessed that wonderful attribute of blistering pace that was valued by colleagues and feared by opposing defenders in equal measure. He did have weaknesses, of course. He was my regular tennis opponent during my time at Tottenham and, unless my memory is being conveniently selective, I often got the better of Garth. In fact, I'm not sure he ever beat me. But, while hitting the net on a tennis court was a regular source of irritation, his knack of doing exactly that on a football pitch – as he did 22 times in his debut season – made him a popular character at the club.

If you're wondering why I'm lavishing such praise on my old friend, the reason is simple: Garth Crooks claims that I killed his career. And, I have to say, I can see where he's coming from. At the sharp end of the 1980/81 season I stole the limelight from Garth on a night that would otherwise have belonged to him. Twice.

That campaign of 1980/81, my third as a Spurs player, was an unforgettable one for everybody associated with Tottenham Hotspur. The previous two seasons had been something of a struggle. The team was constantly changing – the line-up was often altered after a defeat, of which there were several – the performance levels of individual players varied wildly and, as a result, we failed to establish any sort of consistency. For the first time in my football career, I was going into games without being certain that my team could win.

Some of the signings that Keith made just didn't work out. In Argentina, managers come under a great deal more pressure than in England. In my country, after just a couple of defeats the boss is deemed to be on borrowed time. I'm sure that if a manager had been working under similar circumstances to Keith in Argentina, and his team – complete with two expensively acquired World Cup stars – were producing similar results to ours, then he would probably have been shown the door. Tottenham, of course, kept faith with Keith, and were absolutely right to do so. It was only fair that he was allowed time for his foreign additions to settle into the side. We lost many games during my first two seasons at Spurs, but Keith impressed me with the way he handled defeat. If he criticised anyone he did it in a reasonable manner, preferring to address us collectively rather than picking out individuals. That approach, I believe, helped create a sense of solidarity in the dressing room. Keith wanted to nurture a strong team spirit, and didn't want to damage that by highlighting individual errors in front of the whole squad. For example, if a team concedes a goal from a corner, the easiest thing to do is to point the finger of blame at whoever was meant to be marking the goalscorer. Keith, however, would suggest that a teammate could have spotted the goalscorer running free of his marker and should maybe have left his own man to help out. I think this is the very essence of team spirit.

Gradually things began to improve and after a while Keith got it right. I think he always had a vision of his side playing neat, attacking football. Tottenham were renowned for doing things with a certain flourish, thanks to their championship-winning teams of the past, and Keith was intent on extending that tradition. Getting a team to play attractive, winning football is far easier said than done, however. You have to be patient, you have to find the right blend of players and you have to trust those players. It doesn't happen overnight. When we first arrived at Tottenham we found a club that was newly promoted and desperate to stay in the division. The priority was survival. Results came before all else, including the style in which those results were attained. Due to a fear of losing, the players were not willing to take risks. I could understand that. We weren't the most gifted of sides, and some players were keen to get the ball as far away from our goal as possible as quickly as possible. That whole environment was not conducive to playing beautiful football and the heavy, muddy pitches we often played on hardly helped.

Keith persevered though and eventually found the right balance in a variety of ways – youth and experience, defence and attack, grit and guile. By 1981 we had quality in every position. The goalkeeping duties were shared between Barry Daines, Mark Kendall and Milija Aleksic. Ray Clemence, a fantastic keeper, made the position his own after arriving from Liverpool, but that was a little later. Towards the end of 1980/81 Milija became our number 1. He joined the club at roughly the same time as I did, from Luton Town, and worked hard in training to earn his chance. Although he didn't play that many games for Spurs he came into the side at an exciting time for the club and certainly didn't let us down.

The 'grit' that I mentioned earlier emanated mainly from the heart of our defence, where we possessed a formidable pair of centre halves. Paul Miller, who progressed through the youth system at Tottenham, was a genuine Cockney. 'Maxie' was a real London lad. Partnering him at the back was Graham Roberts, who came to us from non-league Weymouth. He was a bit rough around the edges when he arrived at the club, but it didn't take him long to realise there was more to football than the physical side of it. He developed into a player of such repute that he was capped a handful of times by England.

My goodness, did those boys love to tackle. They only knew how to play one way – 100 per cent fully committed, whether it be a five-a-side game in training or an FA Cup final at Wembley. They weren't fussy – they didn't care who they kicked! When it was raining and the training pitch was covered in mud I found it hard to play my natural game. Those two were in their element though. They loved it, flying into challenges all over the place. Typical defenders. It was the only time they could claim to be the best players on the pitch! I used to say to them, "Why do you like kicking people so much?" They would smile and say, "Come on Ricky . . ." They told me it was a good conditioning exercise for our forwards. That was their excuse anyway.

While both Miller and Roberts were uncompromising in their approach, their styles varied somewhat. They went about their business in different ways, if you like. Big Graham wasn't one to overcomplicate matters. The manner in which he 'welcomed' an opposing striker to the game was totally physical. Bang! Some of those challenges used to make me wince, and I was stood 30 yards away. Goodness knows how those on the receiving end felt. Maxie, on the other hand, was more subtle. More vocal. He never stopped talking to opposing players. Don't get me wrong, he was as tough as they come. He would take anyone on. But he didn't just use physical force when attempting to unsettle the opposition. If we were facing a team whose players weren't so famous, maybe in the

Cup against a side from the lower divisions, he would adopt a particular verbal approach. Standing alongside the striker he was marking, he'd start quizzing the player with a question like "So how much do you earn a week then?" or "What car do you drive?" Alternatively, he might take one puzzled look at his opponent and ask, "How come I've never seen your picture in the newspaper before?" That was usually followed by a glance in Steve Perryman's direction. "STEVE!" he would shout, before pointing at the object of his goading. "WHO THE F*** IS THIS?"

Paul Miller was always trying to break the concentration of any player he came up against. He didn't miss a trick. Like the time we were playing Southampton and Alan Ball became embroiled in a furious argument with his teammate Mick Channon during the game. This was perfect for Maxie. He wasn't about to pass up an opportunity to stoke the fire. He wandered over to Alan Ball and discreetly told him, "You're a World Cup winner, Alan; you can't let him talk to you like that." Moments later he stood next to Mick Channon. "You're an England international, Mick," he whispered. "You're a senior player. Have you heard what he's been saying? I can't believe you're letting him get away with that." That was typical Maxie, always winding opponents up. On this occasion his antics almost saw two of them come to blows. Eventually they caught on and Alan Ball snapped, switching the focus of his anger onto Maxie, which I suppose was exactly the reaction our man was after.

Maxie was the life and soul of the dressing room. He knew everything about everything. He was always talking or cracking jokes, full of confidence. He would sit in the dressing room before a game and say, "Who are we playing today? Who's their best player? I'll mark him. No problem." Whether or not he was always effective in nullifying his target is another matter! But more often than not he was, and much of that was down to his unstinting self-belief.

Together, Graham Roberts and Paul Miller grew in confidence and reached a pinnacle, I would say, in 1981. They were good lads. Like everyone in that team, I had a sound relationship with them. They were very tough competitors, never afraid to put their head in where most would think twice about dangling a foot. I think it may have frustrated them that I didn't compete at the same intensity as they did, but it wasn't in my nature. "It's fine kicking people," I would say, "but we have to go up the other end and try to score at some point." As we sat in the changing room after a game, or later on in the bar, they would review their afternoon's work together, reflecting on every kick and punch in every scrap and tussle. It reminded me of the post-match conversations that my old Argentina teammates Daniel Passarella and Américo Gallego used to have. A typically blunt exchange would go along the lines of:

Gallego: "How many players did you elbow today?"
Passarella: "Two. And you?"
Gallego: "Me? Three."
Passarella: "Nice one."

They were another formidable pair, for the national team and River Plate. With Gallego in central midfield and Passarella behind him at sweeper their philosophy was simple when it came to dealing with the opposition. "If he gets past me then you smash him" was their general understanding.

Regularly occupying the fullback positions in our side of 1981 were two outstanding players. At right back we had our captain Steve Perryman, or 'Mr Tottenham' as I like to call him. If I were asked to pick a Best XI consisting only of my former teammates then I would always find room in the side for Stevie P. He was mechanically perfect. When he first broke into the Tottenham side as a teenager he was a midfielder, before later adapting to a role in defence. He knew exactly how the game worked. I once asked Steve, "How come you did things so simply on the pitch when you had the ability to do so much more?" He explained to me precisely how his mind used to work on the field. "When I received the ball," he said, "the first question I always asked myself was 'Can I go forward?' If not, the second option was to move the ball sideways; if that wasn't possible then I'd go backwards." And there you have it. Pure and simple. The textbook guide to playing at right back. It gave me a real insight into the structured thinking of a defender. I never used to think that methodically. I played on instinct. After that conversation I thought, "Stevie's got it sussed." Steve was a top player who made quick decisions in a match based on a snap assessment of each situation. Most of the time he knew what he was going to do with the ball before he even received it. I, on the other hand, allowed my intuition to lead me. The tag 'Mr Tottenham' came about because, for many years, the name Steve Perryman was synonymous with that of Tottenham Hotspur Football Club. Steve took great pride in his role as skipper. He treated it as a 24-hour job, always making sure he was around and always in early for training. Whether it be the youth team players, the secretary, the tea lady or the supporters, Steve had time for everyone connected with the club. He was the ultimate team player, the ultimate leader and the ultimate professional.

Chris Hughton played on the other side of our defence. With Stevie on the right and Chris on the left we had real pace and solidity on either side of our central defenders. Chris had all the attributes necessary to succeed in his position. A complete player. He was quick, tenacious and – like Steve – extremely difficult to beat. Rarely did an opponent get the better of him. Chris didn't only contribute to the team defensively, though; he offered us an attacking threat as well. He used his blistering pace and enthusiasm to fly up the wing whenever we were in possession. He was always willing to receive the ball, with Glenn Hoddle in particular constantly aware of this. Glenn, of course, was aware of everything on the pitch. A common movement for us would see Glenn switch the play from midfield with a diagonal pass into the path of Chris, striding onto the ball from nowhere high up the pitch. It was an outlet we often utilised and one from which we often profited. Although he wasn't tricky when running at defenders Chris made good use of possession in the final third. There was no need for him to be tricky really – he was a fullback, not a winger. His speed meant he didn't have to be clever when confronted by an opposing player anyway; he just breezed down the line before delivering a cross. They were usually decent crosses too.

With Stevie P and Chris in the side we were really strong in the fullback positions. This was one area in which the team wasn't so accomplished when myself and Ossie first arrived at White Hart Lane. The team as a whole wasn't of the highest standard, I think it's fair to say, even though the professionalism of each individual in the squad was genuinely impressive. We did lack quality in those early days. Some of our defenders weren't the most effective of man-markers. They would scamper forward, neglecting their defensive duties, just to put in a bad cross! During our debut season there were many nights when myself and Ossie would reflect on the day's events. Sometimes we struggled to make any positive assessments. "What on earth was so-and-so trying to do today?" we would wonder. "He had a stinker! What a long road ahead of us!" It wasn't like the Spurs players were any less talented than those we played with in Argentina. Just a bit more naive. In Argentina the defenders didn't extend themselves beyond their capabilities. They knew their limitations. But that wasn't the case with some of the Spurs boys. By 1981, however, Keith had strengthened where necessary. We functioned like a proper team.

Chris was a quiet guy who did everything in the correct manner. And what a thoroughly decent man. I was so pleased to see him find success as manager of Newcastle United, taking them back into the Premier League in his first full season in charge. Chris is a nice guy, a real gentleman. There is a widespread view in football that to be effective as a manager it's essential to shout and scream and generally be aggressive towards everyone. Reassuringly, Chris has dispelled that theory. Nice guys can be successful managers. I told him that – at the same time as offering him my congratulations – when I saw him shortly after he'd taken Newcastle to the Championship title.

So Perryman, Roberts, Miller and Hughton provided us with a solid defensive base. When evaluating the array of talent that starred in front of them, there is only one place to start. Every successful side needs a playmaker and we had one of the very best around: Glenn Hoddle could have played in any team, anywhere, at any time. Apart from Diego Maradona Glenn was the best player I ever played with. His touch was exquisite and his movement was brilliant. His greatest strength though was his vision. He had wonderful awareness. The area on a football pitch around the ball is always so congested, with players from both sides and even the referee in close proximity. The big spaces are always away from the ball on the other side of the pitch, and Glenn was an expert at sensing that. He was an intelligent footballer. I'm not sure I've ever seen a player with such precision – he could play the ball to your foot, or chest, from 30, 40 or 50 yards – and he was a goalscorer too. One season he scored more than 20 times for Spurs. Glenn found the net in a variety of ways, often working himself an opening by playing quick one-twos within shooting distance of our opponents' goal. He converted free kicks and penalties, he scored from long range with stinging drives or spectacular volleys and he could bend the ball into the top corner or chip the keeper. He was a first-class finisher.

It used to amaze me when I heard Glenn being criticised for his performances in the England team, because he supposedly didn't work hard enough, or run far enough or tackle often enough. That wasn't his job. Some people didn't seem to understand that. Other players around him were there to assume those responsibilities and do the dirty work. That's what having a balanced team is all about. Glenn was in the side because he was more gifted than anyone else. I'm not sure that any other player in England could have offered the same level of artistry as he did back then. What more did they want from him? Away from football Glenn was a normal, regular kind of person. When Ossie wasn't around I shared a room with him on a couple of away trips. He was a nice guy. Not the most prominent or involved individual in the group, but popular nonetheless.

Constantly buzzing around Glenn at the heart of our midfield was Ossie. Those two complemented each other perfectly. Glenn had more of an attacking inclination, was an excellent long-range passer and scored more goals. Ossie, meanwhile, played a little further back. He was so alert. Far more alert than I ever was, which is probably why he used to get fouled more often than me. Ossie's reactions were razor sharp, and he resolved complicated situations very quickly. The pace of English football was so frantic. With the focus of that chaos concentrated in the middle of the pitch the ball would fly around that area like a pinball. And so did the tackles too. Ossie saw through all that madness, though. He brought a semblance of order to proceedings by claiming the loose ball and slowing things down. He had a calming influence in that respect, which is a real skill.

As I've already said placing me on the left wing didn't have the desired effect and I was soon shifted into another role as Keith continued to experiment. I never returned to the left wing after that, and there was a major reason why. Keith found someone who was tailor-made for the job.

Like Graham Roberts, Tony Galvin was a player who emerged as an important member of the Spurs team after being plucked from non-league football. He was the sort of player we refer to as a *luchador* ('battler') in Argentina, a tireless runner who spent the entire game motoring up and down the wing. He used to work his socks off in every single match. Which is just as well, seeing as Glenn and I were alongside him in midfield! Tony and Ossie were selfless players who made sacrifices for us, who weren't the most industrious of midfielders. It didn't bother Tony. He could run all day. That remarkable running capacity meant that he could cover the whole flank. He was always willing to help out defensively. Going forward, however, was where he really excelled. I wouldn't say that Tony was particularly graceful or subtle in his approach. He wasn't a tricky dribbler who would weave through defences. That wasn't his style. He was direct and extremely effective, though, performing a key role for the side. Ossie and Glenn, for example, were always benefiting from Tony's forward bursts. The two of them would take the ball from him high up the pitch before further prompting an attack. Or they would play one-twos around the opposing fullback, allowing Tony to race clear and fire in a cross. Sometimes his mobility and movement alone created space that the rest of us could exploit. Tony gave the team an injection of oxygen. He had a big, big heart.

Providing the cutting edge up top were a pair of strikers I've already made reference to, Garth Crooks and Steve Archibald. They were different characters with different qualities but the two of them just clicked as a partnership. Steve was a more complete striker than Garth. More natural I would say. Make no mistake about it, Steve was a top, top player. A brilliant finisher. One of his most impressive assets was his sharpness in the box. He turned so quickly in small confined spaces that he rarely failed to get a shot away, even when he was being tightly marked or was surrounded by a group of defenders. In that respect I would say he was similar to his Scottish compatriot Kenny Dalglish, which is just about the highest compliment you can pay a centre forward – Kenny was incredibly good. In addition to that, Steve also proved himself at Barcelona. His goals made him a big favourite at the Nou Camp, and that feat alone speaks volumes for his ability.

I think Garth had to work harder for his success. He was a real grafter who ultimately gained the rewards that his industry merited. A raw striker when he joined Spurs, Garth gradually learned his craft before developing into one of the division's most dangerous centre forwards. He was at his best when running in behind fullbacks, which brought both himself and the team much joy. That work ethic made him a popular member of the side.

Steve and Garth worked wonderfully well in tandem on the pitch. Off it, they were markedly different personalities. Garth was always impeccably dressed. Very smart, to the point of being quite elegant even. It was an image that he made every effort to uphold. Garth was a bubbly character, so it doesn't surprise me that he's since found success as a TV presenter and pundit. Steve, on the other hand, was more subdued. A nice man, but sometimes very subdued. And he loved to complain! Some days he was talkative but other days he would keep himself to himself.

As well as having a settled line-up at that time Keith also had the luxury of being able to call upon a highly capable pool of reserves when any of the preferred starters were unavailable. A productive youth set-up saw the likes of Ian Crook, Micky Hazard, Mark Falco, Terry Gibson and Garry Brooke develop through the system to emerge as genuine first-team contenders. What I remember about those boys as much as anything else was that they were a really respectful group. Falco went on to score lots of goals at senior level, while Gibson – a frighteningly quick striker – was unlucky not to play as many games as his early promise suggested he might.

Crook was a gifted midfielder and Brooke was a direct replacement for me, even though Garry and I were different types of players. We operated in the same area, but Garry was more of a goalscorer than I was.

For me though – and for many others connected with Tottenham around that time – the pick of that bunch was Micky Hazard. Micky was like a clone of Glenn Hoddle. In terms of natural talent I'd say the two were roughly on a par, which gives a perfect indication of how highly I rated him. With the ability he had Micky should have achieved much more than he did. Why he wasn't an established member of the Spurs side for several years, or a regular England international, is something of a mystery to me and most others who worked alongside him. I saw Micky train every day. He was an exceptional footballer. Maybe there was an issue with his mentality. Maybe he didn't realise how good he was. Perhaps a lack of confidence stifled his progress, preventing him from breaking out of Glenn's shadow. Maybe he just took his talent for granted. Sometimes players don't appreciate that if they make sacrifices and work a little harder they can achieve greatness.

Our training ground at Cheshunt was such a fun place to be. The atmosphere was great, due to a fantastic team spirit. That can happen when you carefully assemble a side, as Keith did, with the inclusion of several young players. There were times when the boys didn't agree on certain issues – we had some strong characters who weren't shy in voicing their opinions – but those situations never escalated into serious arguments. The team included a range of personalities. As I've already said, Paul Miller was always talking, for instance, whereas Steve Archibald would sometimes say nothing at all.

As for me, I was able to savour the camaraderie as my grasp of English improved. I would say it took me around six to eight months to first get a genuine feel for the language, in terms of understanding dialect on the television, making sense of newspapers and having some idea of what was being said in team talks. After two years of lessons with our teacher Matthew I felt even more settled in that respect. In addition to that I listened to the radio in my car and, by doing so, became increasingly familiar with common phrases and the way in which sentences were structured. Learning simple expressions became quite exciting. Ossie picked up the language much quicker than I did. If I hadn't been so lazy, allowing him to translate for me and speak on my behalf much of the time, I would have learned a lot quicker myself.

Although we could only muster another mid-table finish of tenth in 1981 there were encouraging signs that indicated the club was moving in the right direction. Each of the top three sides in the division – title winners Aston Villa, runners-up Ipswich Town and third-placed Arsenal – were all beaten at White Hart Lane, and we completed a home-and-away double over European champions Nottingham Forest. Only three teams exceeded our total of 70 top-flight goals, with Crooks and Archibald claiming more than half of that tally between them. Something exciting was brewing. A title challenge may have been beyond us that term, but a Cup run? Now that was a possibility.

Chapter Twelve
THE ROAD TO WEMBLEY

Almost as soon as I arrived in England I became aware of the FA Cup and its place in football folklore. It was a special competition, an event of great importance to English supporters. There was no equivalent in Argentina – there still isn't – and both Ossie and I were enchanted by its grand history. Only a select few clubs were capable of claiming the league title, but we could all dream about winning the FA Cup.

As for Wembley, we knew our story wouldn't be complete until we played there. When we first moved to Tottenham in 1978 there wasn't a great deal that Ossie or I knew about English football. We knew all about Wembley Stadium though; anyone in Argentina who knows anything about football knows about Wembley Stadium. It's the most iconic arena in England. One of the most famous football grounds in the whole world. Football was born in England, and Wembley is the one place that represents the country's proud footballing history more powerfully than anywhere else. The fact that no club was affiliated to the stadium just added to its mystique. No one could call it home. If we needed any further confirmation of the importance attached to reaching Wembley then we only had to listen to our colleagues chatting amongst themselves in the Tottenham dressing room. It was such a big deal. They were desperate to get there. Some of the game's greatest players never got the opportunity to play at Wembley. We figured there were two ways we could make it there. One was with the national team, which was unlikely seeing as (a) England had to first arrange a friendly at home to Argentina and (b) we then had to be selected for it. The prospect of that particular option coming to fruition was even more bleak for me than it was for Ossie, who – unlike myself – continued to receive international recognition after leaving Argentina. Our other potential route to Wembley was via a Cup final with Spurs. So that's what we set our sights on. If we didn't play at Wembley, we soon realised, then something would for ever be missing from our English experience. We *had* to play there.

I think it's a real shame that a major knockout competition similar to the FA Cup doesn't exist in Argentina. Sadly, I doubt if there will ever be such a tournament contested in my country, although I'm not sure why. That's disappointing really. There are Cups on offer in all the leading European countries. Italy have the Coppa Italia, Spain the Copa del Rey. Germany and France have their own Cup competitions too. In some countries, like England, there are two. Let's face it, only a small percentage of professional footballers become domestic champions. For many, the experience of even challenging for the title is a rarity. Some – several in fact – will go through their whole careers without so much as a sniff of the major prize. The Cup offers these players an alternative path to glory. A realistic opportunity of picking up some silverware.

What the Cup also does is spice up the domestic season. There's nothing quite like it for drama and excitement. The FA Cup is a wonderful competition that is responsible for producing some of the English game's most memorable moments. From the lower reaches of semi-professional football to the very top of the Premier League, hundreds of clubs take part. Even little non-league teams can claim to be participating in the same competition as the likes of Manchester United and Liverpool. Every year the small clubs dream of playing against a Premier League giant, and every year that dream comes true for someone.

There's so much more to the FA Cup than just winning it. I love the romanticism. Steve Perryman is director of football at Exeter City and a few years ago they played Manchester United at Old Trafford in the FA Cup. They forced a replay too. What a moment in the history of that football club, and what an unforgettable time for their supporters. Not to mention the financial windfall that such a tie brings. I would imagine drawing a big club in the FA Cup can generate enough money to help sustain a small club for some time. It's like hitting the jackpot. It would be brilliant if a similar thing happened in Argentina. Imagine the great Boca Juniors or River Plate travelling to play a tiny club like Deportivo Morón. The local people would go crazy.

One of the most exciting features of the FA Cup for me was the draw. I remember how all the players used to huddle around the radio at training on a Monday lunchtime and listen as each name was announced. The initial priority, of course, was to claim home advantage. If our number did come out first, meaning the tie would take place at White Hart Lane, a collective gasp would follow. "Tottenham Hotspur

. . ." then a hush . . . "will play . . ." The silence lasted as long as it took the FA dignitaries to reveal the identity of our opponents. Whether the reaction was a relieved cry of "Yes!" or a deflated groan depended on the status of the club we'd been drawn to face.

We had a decent run in the competition in each of my first two years at Tottenham. We got as far as the quarter-finals both times, before losing to Manchester United and Liverpool respectively. Ossie scored a memorable winner away to Manchester United during the early rounds of our 1980 campaign, and having made no secret of his desire to play at Wembley, was fast developing a close association with the FA Cup.

The draw in 1981 was, I must say, kind to us. After needing a replay to see off second division QPR, we were drawn at home to Hull City (Third Division), Coventry City (first division) and then Exeter City (Third Division). Those three White Hart Lane fixtures were negotiated relatively comfortably and, all of a sudden, we were one game from Wembley. It actually took us two games to get there, but it was well worth the wait.

Hillsborough was the venue for our semi-final, with fellow top-flight side Wolverhampton Wanderers providing the opposition. I'd missed the first three months of 1981 due to injury, but came off the bench and impressed sufficiently in helping us claim a 2-2 draw with Everton one week before the Wolves game to earn a starting spot at Hillsborough. On reflection – I'm really not sure that I appreciated it at the time – my selection for such an important game was a prime example of how Keith did believe in me, even if I was sometimes convinced otherwise. That same belief, of course, would eventually pay glorious dividends.

On a tense afternoon at Hillsborough, Wolves scored a contentious last-minute penalty to square the game at 2-2 and take it into extra-time. Glenn made a well-timed sliding tackle in the area but instead of awarding a corner the referee Clive Thomas pointed to the spot. Unbelievable. It wasn't a complete surprise though. Clive Thomas was just about the only British referee we'd heard of in Argentina, thanks to a highly controversial decision he made during the 1978 World Cup. Back then, at the end of a group match between Brazil and Sweden, Zico headed in a corner to secure what would have been a 2-1 win for Brazil. Thomas didn't allow the goal to stand though, after blowing his whistle for full-time while the ball was on its way into the box. As you can imagine, the Brazilians weren't impressed. At Hillsborough he was back in the spotlight after making another hotly disputed decision. Psychologically, having been so close to sealing our place in the final, that late equaliser dealt us a crushing blow. Extra-time seemed to last for ever and we just about held on for a replay. Wolves really stretched us in that added period and I had serious concerns ahead of the second game. I remember thinking that if Wolves played like that again then we would be in big trouble. What I didn't envisage, however, was the state of euphoria that would engulf Highbury four days later.

The home of our north London rivals Arsenal was chosen to host the replay. I'm still not entirely sure why. FA Cup semi-finals were traditionally held at neutral venues, normally a fair distance from each of the participating clubs and, ideally, somewhere in between. Villa Park, for example, often hosted semi-finals when a team from the north was drawn against one from the south. For our initial semi-final meeting with Wolves we both headed north to Sheffield. It was closer to Wolves'

Midlands base than ours, but neutral all the same. Playing at Highbury, on the other hand, gave us a huge advantage. We could have walked there! It was right on our doorstep – it may have taken me a little while to find my way around London, but even I knew that. Maybe it was fate. The FA Cup draw hadn't taken us out of London until our semi-final trip to Hillsborough. We'd been pulled out of the hat first on three occasions, with the one exception sending us across town to play Queens Park Rangers in the third round. Now we were back in the capital. I'm not sure how the powers that be came to their decision when choosing a venue for the replay, but we certainly weren't going to contest it. And neither were the masses of Tottenham fans who jumped at the chance of making the home of their great rivals their very own for the night.

I'm not sure how many games I clocked up during my career as a footballer. Several hundred at least. Some days I was good, some days I was bad. Some games I enjoyed, others I didn't. But only a few of those appearances left a lasting mark on my memory like that night at Highbury. I must say it wasn't usually my favourite ground to play at. From very early on I was made aware by my colleagues, and anyone else associated with Spurs come to think of it, of just how important the north London derbies were. If we could only beat one team in a whole season then the supporters demanded that it be Arsenal. Those games were so frenetic. The atmosphere was intense, with both sets of fans fired up and full of aggression. That transmitted to the pitch, where the games often degenerated into nothing more than a physical battle. It just seemed to be a case of crash-bang-wallop as the tackles flew in from all angles. Sometimes, just occasionally, a football match would break out. It was all too tense really.

On the night we played Wolves though, Highbury was a wonderful place to be. On emerging from the tunnel all you could see – covering three-quarters of the stadium at least – was a sea of blue and white. And the noise was incredible. With that support behind us we were convinced we would win. We couldn't lose. It was vibrant, loud, exciting. What an atmosphere. *Electric* just about comes close to doing it justice. Energised by our fervent following, we streamed forward from the start. We seemed to create a chance with every attack. Everyone was passing the ball well, and it was one of those occasions when everything just clicked. Garth scored twice, giving us the lead with a header before racing onto an exquisite pass from Glenn to make it 2-0 at the break. Then I trumped him by claiming a goal that some people tell me was the finest I ever scored in a Tottenham shirt.

The game had come to something of a standstill by the time I received the ball in a wide right position, deep inside the Wolves half. I cut inside and, 25 yards from goal, thought, "Why not?" From a young age I was comfortable shooting with either foot so, with the target in range, I took a swing with my left leg. The subsequent contact was so sweet. The ball flew in a straight line, giving the goalkeeper no chance as it whistled inside the far post. There was a second before it went in when I could see for sure that I'd scored, and that the stadium was just about to erupt. That feeling is priceless. The game finished 3-0 and we were off to Wembley. I remember that as being a very, very happy night for everyone connected with the club. The dressing room was so vibrant. It was a top, top moment.

Just making it to the final marked some kind of achievement for Spurs, and particularly so for us Argentinians. After the club signed two foreign players with big reputations for a big fee the expectation levels at White Hart Lane rose by a big margin too. Clinching a place in the Cup final gave us a perfect chance to relieve that weight of expectation from our shoulders. For Keith too, it was a pivotal time. He was within striking distance of claiming the major trophy that would finally justify his extravagant spending spree of 1978.

Chapter Thirteen
REDEMPTION

The thing about scoring the winning goal in an FA Cup final is that you never get tired of talking about it. Ever. My moment came against Manchester City in 1981 in a final that illustrated perfectly the inconsistency that plagued my career as a footballer. Very good or very bad, that was me. Never inbetween. I've often spoken to Ossie about my fluctuating form. In his book he describes me as a special player . . . but how there were some days when he had trouble believing I was even a professional. I'm not sure why I was like that. In Argentina we have a saying which, roughly translated, means 'It depends how we wake up'. Some days I felt good, sharp and alert. Other days I didn't. I just don't think I was conditioned to work at my maximum level every single day. Growing up as a child I helped my father around the farm, but things were done at a different pace. I wasn't used to working at a high intensity all the time. It wasn't in my nature.

I never quite became attuned to the day-to-day demands of English football. Sometimes, in five-a-side games at training, I didn't even move. Peter Shreeve, our coach, would come over to me and say, "Is everything OK, Ricky?" And I would say, "Yes. Everything's fine." Don't get me wrong, I'm not proud of my sluggish approach to training. Years later I realised for myself just how frustrating such players can be for a manager. The problem was I couldn't seem to change.

At Tottenham the principles of training were instilled by the legendary manager Bill Nicholson, long before I turned up at the club. He insisted his players adopt the same approach to every single game, be it on the training pitch or in a competitive match situation. 'Train as you play' was his maxim. He demanded the same level of intensity from his players in every single session. That way, he reasoned, his team were guaranteed to perform at the desired tempo when match day came around. The results of this policy are, of course, embedded in Tottenham folklore.

I would never dream of questioning the great man's ideals. Bill Nicholson is the figure around which the most glorious passage in the history of Tottenham Hotspur revolves. His was a different mentality to the one that I was used to, however. A very English mentality that still existed when I joined Spurs. To illustrate that difference I would point to the manner in which Diego Maradona used to train. In truth, he did very little on the training ground. He practised free kicks, joined in *loquito* (the 'two-in-the-middle' warm-up drill) and played a bit of five-a-side. Yet he was still the greatest player in the world. By the same token, it would be interesting to know how hard Lionel Messi works between games. I'm not saying that either approach is right or wrong. They just involve alternative ways of thinking. Whenever I saw someone score a hat-trick in training I would think, "Save it for a proper match!" I didn't want to leave my best work on the practice pitch. Having a bad game used to upset me, not a bad training session.

Regardless of my application in training, or lack of it, I started virtually every game up to Christmas in 1980/81. Injury then kept me out of the reckoning until later that term, but I returned to the side right on cue to play my part in a pulsating conclusion to the campaign. The time between walking off the pitch at the end of our semi-final replay victory against Wolves at Highbury and the day of the FA Cup final was an extraordinary period. It was thrilling. Utterly memorable. To put the situation in perspective, Tottenham had not won the FA Cup, or even reached the final, since 1967. Spurs fans had been forced to wait 14 long years to see their team land another shot at the domestic game's most prestigious knockout prize. In addition to that, they'd suffered much despair in the interim. Tottenham did enjoy League Cup and UEFA Cup success in the early 1970s, but Bill Nicholson vacated his post soon after and the club fell from grace at an alarming rate. Relegation in 1977 represented the lowest point in Tottenham's recent history. By 1981 that had all been buried in the past, though. A club with a grand tradition in the Cup – stretching back to the beginning of that century and reinforced by the legendary side of the 1960s – was off to Wembley once again. Spurs supporters regarded the occasion as a symbol of their club's re-emergence. They felt they were back. The anticipation was incredible. Total euphoria.

The bulk of that three or four week spell prior to the final was a wonderfully happy, carefree time. Nearer the match, there's no doubt that we began to feel the pressure. The Cup final is only a truly memorable occasion if you win it, after all. But to begin with we were content to relax, soak up the atmosphere and enjoy the prospect of a big day out at Wembley. Just taking a walk around the area where I lived was a delight during the Cup final build-up. Everyone, and I mean everyone, wanted to wish us well. Our neighbours, who up to that point had greeted us with a simple "Hello" or "Good morning" with typical English politeness, put their reservedness to one side by rushing over to shake our hands and discuss the forthcoming final. Wherever we went the people reacted in the same manner. Whether it be on the street, at the post office or in the butcher's shop, cries of "Come on you Spurs!" followed us everywhere. Understandably, the fans could not control their excitement. It was fantastic.

Having said all that, my own feelings leading up to the final were actually quite mixed due to a situation that had developed off the pitch, a situation that had left me fearing for my future in fact. The three-year contract I signed when I joined Tottenham in the summer of 1978 was about to expire as the FA Cup final approached. A new deal was on the table but the terms were far from satisfactory. In truth, it was a pretty derisory offer.

Ossie's contract was also up for renewal at the same time. Unlike me, he was happy with the proposed terms of his new deal. That was because, unlike me, he'd been made a lucrative offer. I was disappointed. Club officials at Tottenham knew how close the two of us were. They knew there was every chance we would discuss the finer details of our respective offers, and that I would discover the considerable disparity between the two. It wasn't like they were trying to hide the fact they didn't value me as highly as Ossie. I'll be the first to admit that Ossie adapted to the English game quicker than I did, and showed greater consistency. He was an outstanding servant for Spurs. But the situation seemed quite clear to me.

Tottenham were willing to let me go. I sensed the club weren't all that bothered about keeping me, and that I'd be looking for a new team that summer. The Cup final, I thought, would probably be my last game for Tottenham Hotspur.

It was impossible to get too downbeat though, considering the furore that was going on around me as the big match drew closer. And it wasn't just the supporters who were whipping themselves into a frenzy. The excitement was just as palpable in our dressing room as it was on the terraces. It's no wonder we didn't win any of our remaining league matches after victory over Wolves had confirmed our place in the final. Keith rested some key players in the last couple of games as we completed our league programme. But it's fair to say that only one match seriously occupied our thoughts at that stage, regardless of the manager's team selection.

We were counting down the days to the final. What better way could there possibly be to wrap up a season? It's all we were talking about. It meant so much to the boys, especially the ones who hadn't played international football. They couldn't wait to walk out at Wembley. For some it was a rare opportunity. Just ask Stevie P how much it meant. Even now he speaks of that FA Cup venture with a passion that has not diminished in the slightest over the decades that have since passed.

The fact that our meeting with Manchester City in 1981 was the 100th FA Cup final just added to the prestige of the occasion. The Football Association, rightly proud of the landmark, made sure of that. The media, as one would expect, also went into overdrive. The FA Cup is so special, there was a certain uniqueness about the situation. Due to the absence of a cup competition in Argentina the closest thing to a one-off

final that we ever witnessed was a play-off for the championship title. When that happened the press went crazy, but it
still wasn't quite like the FA Cup final. Nothing is, or at least
it wasn't back then. I have to say the English press were generally much better behaved than their Argentine counterparts.
The whole media approach was more orderly in England.
Journalists attended formal press conferences to obtain their
copy ahead of the game. We certainly weren't hounded or
made to feel as though the press were suffocating us, despite
the enormity of the situation. The media were very respectful
of the players.

The build-up to the game provided me with yet another series
of new experiences, one of which took me a while to fully
comprehend. In fact, it still puzzles me even now. "Come on
Ricky, we're off to record a song for the Cup final," I was told
one day. A song? Us? Singing? Just when I thought I was getting
to grips with the English language I was given that mystifying
nugget of information to unravel. Surely my understanding of
the language had failed me. "They can't seriously want me to
sing," I thought. "Make a record? Why on earth would we do
that?"

Before I knew it the whole squad was standing in a recording
studio with Chas 'n' Dave. Surreal? Just a bit. I was expecting
the Cup final to spark an increased level of media interest,
with more press conferences, interviews and photo shoots.
But this I wasn't expecting. And just when I thought I'd heard
it all they told me that Ossie would be the lead singer. What?!
I couldn't stop laughing. He's more tone deaf than I am! And
I've got a terrible voice. Thank goodness I wasn't given a solo
line to deliver. I couldn't even come in on cue when we were
all singing the chorus.

It's traditional, I was informed, to release a Cup final song. *Ossie's Dream* was the title, which is still remembered with great fondness by Tottenham supporters to this day. They still sing it when Spurs go on a decent Cup run now. "In the Cup for Tott-ing-ham" was Ossie's line. He was petrified! Mind you, you wouldn't know it now. I've never known anyone to hog the microphone at karaoke as much as Ossie does. And his voice still hasn't improved.

Lo and behold, the song was a revelation. We could now list "chart success" next to "World Cup winner" on our CVs. Not that I really understood what was going on. We even sang on *Top of the Pops*, which was all a bit embarrassing for me. I was rubbing shoulders with genuine musicians. Some of them were world-famous rock stars. And then there was us, a group of tuneless footballers, competing against them with our song! It was all great fun really.

I remember feeling full of excitement in the days leading up to the match. After being measured up for our suits – another Cup final tradition – we stayed in the countryside in the quaint Ponsbourne Park Hotel, which was an ideal location for finalising our big-game preparations. The BBC were fantastic. They organised a TV link-up from Argentina, where they gathered our families in a studio and sat us in front of a screen so we could see them. Ossie joked that he didn't recognise his family. We spoke to them for a few minutes, and the whole operation was quite innovative back then. I chatted with my mother and father, and it was an emotional exchange. It made me feel extremely proud. Finding out that the game was being broadcast live in Argentina merely added to the sense of occasion.

All of a sudden, 24 days after beating Wolves to book our

place in the FA Cup final, the match was upon us. No more build-up, no more interviews, no more *Top of the Pops*. No more talking. It was time for action. For me, that trip to Wembley on 9th May 1981 wasn't my first visit to the famous old stadium. I'd already been there to watch England play Czechoslovakia three years earlier. Wembley was just how I'd imagined it would be. I'd played in some wonderful stadiums like the Bernabeu in Madrid but Wembley was something else. It was totally different. It had a mystique that was unmatched anywhere else. Despite planning extensively for the final I'm not sure that anything can quite prepare a player for his first game at Wembley. Even if that player, like me, had visited the ground as a spectator beforehand. I felt fine on the morning of the game. In the dressing room I was relaxed too. I always was. There are a variety of pre-match routines in every changing room. Some players get uptight and nervous, while others will listen to music in a bid to lift themselves for the game. Some just shout and scream. My general pre-match demeanour never really changed. I was just as laid-back then as when I was sitting down reading a newspaper in my armchair at home.

Cup final day wasn't like any other day though. I walked out of the tunnel a couple of hours before kick-off in my suit for the traditional pre-match stroll around the pitch and, all of a sudden, it hit me: the whole atmosphere, the banners in the crowd, the buzz of anticipation, the global attention. I was in awe of the occasion. Everything about the experience was different from what we'd become accustomed to. We never used to walk around the pitch in our suits and smart shoes before the match, for one. That pitch, incidentally, was in immaculate condition, which only added to the attraction

With Cristina and Ossie, ready to embark on our big adventure after landing at Heathrow Airport in the summer of 1978. Ossie's wife Sylvia, who was heavily pregnant, joined us in England after the birth.

Standing in our new home, pictured for the first time in a Tottenham kit.

Teammates Steve Perryman and John Pratt look as bemused as anyone during our official presentation at White Hart Lane.

The stunning story of two World Cup winners joining newly-promoted Tottenham made headlines at home and abroad.

DAILY EXPRESS Tuesday July 11 1978

EXPRESS EXCLUSIVE

SPURS SCOOP THE WORLD

Ardiles and Villa sign in £750,000 double deal

By Malcolm Folley

TOTTENHAM manager Keith Burkinshaw yesterday signed two of Argentina's all-conquering national side — Osvaldo Ardiles and Ricardo Villa — in a £750,000 deal.

Ardiles masterminded Argentina's World Cup triumph in Buenos Aires last month.

Don't forget the camera... and you wont forget the weekend.

Here on Sunday

Burkinshaw buys Argentine stars

Intelligent

TURN TO PAGES 29 AND 31

La presencia de Ardiles y Villa en el Club Tottenham

LONDRES (De un enviado especial). — Aquí, en Inglaterra, el fútbol se siente de una manera muy particular.

Los argentinos Villa y Ardiles junto con el manager de Tottenham

The City Ground, 19th August 1978: Preparing to make my debut for Tottenham.

Ossie adapted quickly to our new environment.

A dream start: I swerve past the Nottingham Forest and England goalkeeper Peter Shilton...

… before converting from close range to mark my first game with a goal.
It was a rare moment of joy in those early days.

I really should have paid more attention during our English lessons; my struggle to understand the language was a major problem.

Enjoying a laugh with Ossie and Tottenham manager Keith Burkinshaw.

Commercial appeal: anyone want to buy a second hand car? We were introduced to the marketing world in England... although we were hardly up to David Beckham's standard!

An early appearance in the blue and white of Tottenham Hotspur.

With Cristina, Ossie, his wife Sylvia and their eldest son Pablo at the house we shared in Chigwell.

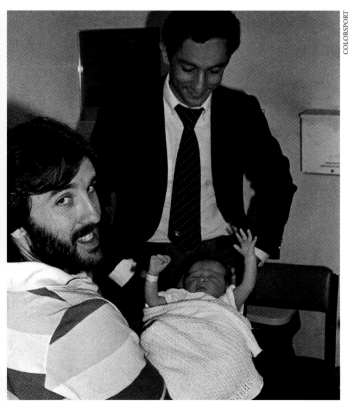

Ossie got lost driving us to the hospital for the birth of Maria Eugenia! Luckily we just about made it in time.

Trudging off the pitch after being substituted in the 1981 FA Cup final, I could have no idea how different life would feel five days later.

The goal that changed my life.

Let the celebrations begin: basking in the glory with Glenn Hoddle...

...my great friend Ossie...

...and parading the famous old trophy.

Showing off my FA Cup winner's medal with my eldest daughter, María Eugenia.

The 1982 FA Cup final came at a difficult and unhappy time in my life, during the Falklands War. Because of the high profile nature of the match it was felt that I shouldn't play so I watched us win the trophy from the bench.

Trying our best to look the part outside White Hart Lane.

Country boy: I took my hunting instincts with me to England.

Standing in the centre of the back row as the boss of Defensa y Justicia, the club with whom I began my managerial career.

Back in the colours of Racing, in a friendly that marked the club's centenary in 2003. Facing me - with his distinctive mop of blond hair - is my former Deportivo Cali teammate Carlos Valderrama.

Meet the Villas... Left to right: Ricky, María Eugenia, our granddaughter Julia, Martina, Cristina, myself and Mariana.

Brazil, France, Holland, Italy, Barcelona, Bayern Munich... they all feature in my collection of shirts.

Back in the saddle: Keeping the cattle under control on my farm.

Once a gaucho, always a gaucho: me in my natural habitat.

of playing at Wembley. It was reassuring to discover a surface so flat and true, even if it did mean there would be no excuses for a bad touch. The bright sunshine that traditionally accompanies Cup final day was absent on this occasion, though, as the weather remained distinctly grey throughout and the damp conditions provided the grass with a slick finish.

I remember standing in the centre circle chatting to my teammates surrounded by 100,000 spectators, an enormous crowd that included my sister Noemí and her husband Chacho, who had flown over from Argentina for the game. The terraces were packed to the rafters, the supporters were in full voice long before kick-off and the noise was amazing. And it was all happening in such a magnificent, historic arena. At that point I didn't feel like a footballer. I felt like a member of the public, an ordinary fan who had sneaked in to witness at first hand what this momentous day was all about. It was impossible not to appreciate the magnitude of the occasion.

Having completed our final pre-match preparations we again emerged from the tunnel shortly before three o'clock, this time in two orderly lines behind our respective managers. A deafening crescendo of noise greeted our arrival. We walked over to the touchline and lined up shoulder to shoulder. We met the dignitaries. We warmed up a little more. We stripped off our tracksuit tops and took our positions for the start of the game. The whistle sounded. The match began. It was the perfect stage on which to perform but the worst possible stage on which to fail. Unfortunately, I failed to perform.

I let the biggest game of my life pass me by. I didn't play well at all. As a team, we didn't play well at all. Thankfully we did salvage something from the match though. It could have been – and nearly was – so much worse.

Manchester City had finished just below us in mid-table that season, so there was very little to choose between the two teams. A tense, hard-fought 1-1 draw at Wembley illustrated that point. It was a real battle. I would say we were more of a footballing side than City, but they had some extremely good players nonetheless. In fairness they dominated the game. Their tactics were to smother us in midfield, denying Glenn, Ossie and myself the time and space necessary to dictate proceedings. That's how they felt they could win the match and their plan very nearly worked too. One of their midfielders, Gerry Gow, epitomised their approach. He worked incredibly hard, constantly harassing us and snapping into tackles. By fair means or foul – some of his challenges fell into the latter category – he did an effective job in breaking up the play. We found it difficult to keep the ball and even more difficult to create any decent chances. Whenever we did carve out an opening their goalkeeper Joe Corrigan kept us at bay. He was an excellent keeper whose tally of England caps would almost certainly have been greater had he not played in the same era as Peter Shilton and Ray Clemence. For us no one performed particularly well, although Ossie and Steve Perryman each made important contributions that day. They kept battling away in the hope that things would eventually turn in our favour.

As for me, I just couldn't get into the game. I rarely found myself in possession and almost felt as though I didn't participate at all. I've never looked for excuses, though. As a team we were disappointing, but I personally didn't do anything to influence the match. It's not easy to be creative, or to score goals. That was my job, though. I was in the side to make things happen in the final third, and I failed to deliver. In general, if I was struggling to get on the ball during a match then I struggled to contribute. I was quite a cold player, in the sense that I never used to run around furiously sliding into tackles. Even if I was playing poorly I didn't tear about all over the place in an attempt to show the supporters how hard I was trying. I just didn't seem capable of doing that. Mind you, when I later became a manager I urged my players to demonstrate a high level of commitment even if they were having a bad game. "Show the fans you're making an effort" I told them, as hypocritical as that might sound. On two or three occasions during the Cup final I simply got lost in my own thoughts. I dwelt on the situation, which only added to my frustration. My involvement was minimal. Midway through the second half, with Manchester City leading 1-0, Keith decided it was time to make a change.

Teams were only allowed to have one substitute on the bench back then. That single reserve was often an attacking 'impact' player who could go on and alter the course of a game. Our sub was Garry Brooke, who played as a kind of second striker. Withdrawing me was the only option Keith had really. Replacing either Steve Archibald or Garth Crooks wouldn't have been appropriate. They never stopped running and were always likely to pinch a goal, as they'd already done more than 20 times each that season. Plus the pair of them played further up the pitch than me. I was like an additional forward. On top of all that, let's not forget, I was having a bit of a shocker. My worst fears were confirmed when I reluctantly glanced over to the touchline and saw my number being raised. After 68 minutes my Cup final experience was over.

I was devastated. Devastated, first of all, to be taken off.

Even when I was playing badly I always felt I had the potential to produce a moment that could change the face of a game, with a decisive pass or a flash of skill. Devastated because, with time running out, we were heading for defeat. And devastated because I'd had a poor game when it really mattered. I was so sad. Angry. Acting on instinct, I opted against joining the rest of the Tottenham staff on the bench, and instead headed straight for the tunnel. That long walk with my head bowed was captured on television, in a famous sequence that has since been shown almost as often as the goal that eventually decided the tie five days later. When I look at those television pictures now, with the cameras following me all the way to the dressing room, I must admit I feel pretty sorry for myself. I cut such a dejected figure.

It was all so depressing. This was the centenary FA Cup final. I knew the game was being shown in Argentina, with my family and friends glued to their TV sets back home. I'd spoken to my mother and father via a satellite link-up before the match. My sister and my brother-in-law had travelled thousands of miles just to come and watch me play. And I'd let them all down. Latin people, you must understand, are very emotional people. I was wrong to walk off – I should have sat on the bench and supported the team. But, in truth, I just wanted to get back inside the changing room and cry.

There were one or two tears, but my pain was eased by the sound of a huge roar shortly after I'd returned to the dressing room. Our kitman Johnny Wallis, who was there with me, rushed outside before reappearing with news that Glenn's deflected free kick had drawn us level. Neither side could muster a decisive goal in extra time. We'd got away with it. Despite playing well below our best the FA Cup was still within our reach. Attributing the blame for our disappointing display to one individual would have been unfair. I had a poor game but it's not like I blatantly gave a goal away, or needlessly chopped someone down in the box. We all recognised that the team as a unit failed to function.

My decision to trudge off may not have gone down too well – understandably so – but I was just relieved that we hadn't lost. And at least I re-emerged from the dressing room to watch extra-time from the bench. Keith had a big decision to make, though. Team selection for the initial game had been a relatively straightforward process. There weren't any major issues. But a lacklustre performance at Wembley, from me in particular, gave Keith plenty to think about. Would he take another chance on me in the replay, or would he opt for Garry Brooke, the player who'd just replaced me? Thankfully, the final say didn't rest with Steve Perryman. Stevie was disappointed with my display, and has since admitted approaching Keith after the game to suggest that he should seriously consider leaving me out for the second match. Keith saw things differently, though. Apparently he told me immediately after the 1-1 draw that I would be in the side when we returned to Wembley on the Thursday. I say apparently because my head was so muddled at that point I honestly can't remember what anyone said to me. Call it good man-management, or just good luck, but that decision to back me was pivotal on more than one level. It went some way to determining the outcome of the FA Cup final that year. And it went a long way to determining my legacy: if Keith had left me out, I'm not sure if anyone would be interested in reading my story right now.

And that's the great thing about football. There's always

another game. The most important match? The next one. Life goes on. I tried to forget about my performance in the final, which wasn't too difficult. We had Sunday off before training well on the Monday and Tuesday. You could sense a far more relaxed atmosphere among the group. Prior to the first game, Wembley had carried a certain mystique for the bulk of our players. Steve Perryman had played there in League Cup finals, and Glenn had performed at the famous old stadium whilst on England duty. Apart from that, though, the experience of walking out at 'the Home of Football' was a brand new one for us. With that done we knew what to expect in the replay. Wembley was no longer an unknown factor.

There is no doubt in my mind that, even if he did reassure me of my place straight after the first game, Keith must have seriously questioned whether or not I should start the replay. There were a number of factors to consider, namely the ease with which Manchester City had got amongst us and disrupted our rhythm in the first meeting. In my experience the manager of any side generally has seven or eight preferred players he will always pick, with the remaining three or four spots on the team up for grabs. I always felt as though I was among the three or four 'maybes' in Keith's mind. In the end Keith kept faith with his original line-up. A brave decision perhaps, but he trusted us not to let ourselves down a second time. I think he felt confident the team was too good to do that. Just in case the manager was having doubts about my inclusion I made a concentrated effort during those days before the replay to demonstrate a real desire to retain my place. I thought to myself, "Don't get annoyed because you were substituted; just work hard in training to prove you're desperate to play in the replay." Whether or not that attitude had any specific bearing on Keith's selection dilemma I don't know, but when Thursday night came around I was indeed named in the starting line-up.

There was a renewed sense of confidence within the camp leading up to the replay. On our return to Wembley Peter Shreeve, who was always very supportive of me, decided upon a novel way of lifting my spirits. He tells a story about a plan he devised in order to boost my confidence ahead of the game. During the warm-up he told me to go and stand on the other side of the splendidly dressed marching band that played before the Cup final every year. Peter stayed where he was and instructed me to chip the ball over the band to him. I told him he must be joking. Hadn't he seen my performance at the weekend? "We could be putting those band members in serious danger," I thought. "Come on," he said. "It won't be a problem for someone of your ability." Hardly conventional but it didn't do any harm, either to my confidence or – thankfully – the marching band.

I was under pressure in that second game, no doubt about it. I knew that my poor showing in the initial match probably meant that I had 45 minutes – maximum – to perform in the replay or my night would be over. Garry Brooke, our only substitute, was a more than able reserve. Keith showed in the first game that he was prepared to throw 'Buddha' on if things weren't working out for us. He trusted him and rightly so. Garry had showed a lot of promise that season and was very much in the reckoning for a starting place in the replay. He was a really good player. More of a goalscorer than me, he was very sharp around the box and had a powerful shot. A very clean striker of the ball. We were different players, but we did operate in similar areas of the pitch. Consequently, I was the most likely player to make way if Garry was sent on.

I felt much sharper than I had in the initial game, both physically and mentally. A few minutes after kick-off I was feeling even better. It was a dream situation. Ossie created an opening, Steve Archibald had a shot blocked by Joe Corrigan and the ball just fell at my feet. There I was, standing right in front of a gaping goal, about seven or eight yards out, with the grounded keeper stranded. Time seemed to stand still for a second. The goal seemed enormous. I was about to score in the Cup final. I lashed the ball in and we were 1-0 up.

It was the ideal start for me and my team, as we showed no signs of the sluggishness that had blighted our performance a few days earlier. The celebrations had barely died down, however, when City scored an unbelievably good goal to equalise. Events further down the line may have overshadowed it, but I can't imagine Wembley has ever witnessed many better technical strikes than the effort Steve MacKenzie conjured up that night. The ball was half-cleared from our area and dropped to MacKenzie about 25 yards from goal. With a first-time volley he made the sweetest connection to send the ball flying into the top corner. It was a brilliant goal, but one that has become something of a forgotten gem due to the eventual outcome of the match.

We were back to 1-1 again, just like the first game, although the pulsating nature of the contest suggested it wouldn't stay that way for long. Sure enough, a third goal was scored shortly after half-time. It came at the wrong end as far as we were concerned though, as Paul Miller and Chris Hughton combined to halt a Dave Bennett run and Kevin Reeves converted the resulting penalty. Despite being 2-1 down, the thought of losing the game never entered my mind. We were playing too well for that happen. The transformation in the way we played from the first match to the second was remarkable. In the initial game City had taken a stranglehold in midfield and we struggled to assert our natural tempo. None of our boys could say they played particularly well. The replay was a completely different game though. We were more confident, more relaxed, more assured on the ball. Glenn, Stevie, Ossie, Garth, Tony Galvin and Chris Hughton – everyone was on top form. My own performance was much improved too. Lifted by that early goal I was more influential, more involved than the first game. I wasn't about to make another early exit; I was in it for the duration this time. One of *the* great Cup finals was unfolding as Garth snatched a goal to make it 2-2.

I never get bored of discussing what happened next. Even when I visit England now, people stop me in the street to ask about it. Not just Spurs fans, but Manchester United, Liverpool and even Arsenal supporters. I respect every one of them, so I'm always happy to oblige. Their genuine interest means a lot to me.

I scored a great goal in a great place. If you listen to Tony Galvin, however, he feels he deserves a share of the credit too. He claims he made the goal. Technically he did provide the assist, having transported the ball from defence to attack with a lengthy run up the pitch before rolling it into my path. All I had to do was dribble past three defenders and beat the goalkeeper. Cue John Motson . . .

John Motson, BBC commentator: *"And now Galvin . . . Spurs have got two to his right . . . and Galvin wants to go on his own . . ."*

When I received the ball from Tony my immediate intention was not to score a goal. Had I put myself under that sort of pressure then I'm not sure I would have scored. Besides, there was still a fair distance between myself and Joe Corrigan's goal. In general, my objective whenever I found myself in possession of the ball was to beat an opponent, because that would draw another defender towards me and create space for a teammate. My other aim was to get inside the penalty area. Once inside the box it was like being in a kind of "safe" zone, where opponents had to think twice about making a challenge. If their timing was just a split second out . . . penalty conceded.

John Motson: *"Villa . . ."*

So I darted directly towards the edge of the area, and the massed ranks of Tottenham supporters behind the goal. All of a sudden, the atmosphere changed. Half the ground was muted with tension, while the other half murmured with excitement. I weaved left and then right as I carefully began to negotiate the obstacles ahead of me. Those winding movements had become second nature to me long before that dramatic night at Wembley. As a kid I spent endless hours alone, honing my skills. I didn't need dynamic figures against which to practise the art of dribbling. I made full use of the environment, jinking and swerving my way through the dense cluster of trees that surrounded my house. Fast forward a couple of decades and it was real-life defenders I had to contend with as opposed to stationary plants. A forest of pale blue shirts through which to navigate. First up was the big central defender Tommy Caton. I went to the left of him. Another opponent, fullback Ray Ranson, appeared immediately. I touched the ball beyond him, to the left again. I needed to be more central. I cut back inside Caton, who had returned for another bite. With every touch, every step that took me nearer the goal, the noise grew louder.

John Motson: *"And still Ricky Villa . . ."*

It seemed as though every single Tottenham supporter was urging me to finish. "SHOOT!" came the collective cry. My teammates, I believe, joined in. Just as I was about to grant them that desperate wish the ball got away from me, delaying my shot for a split second as I was forced to take an extra step. It didn't matter. Maybe it even helped, effectively acting as a dummy that created the slightest of openings in the tightest of areas. I eventually got a shot away. And there was nothing Joe Corrigan could do to stop it.

John Motson: *"What a fantastic run . . . he's scored! . . . Amazing goal by Ricky Villa."*

I was never the quickest of runners. On the contrary, I was actually one of the slowest. That night though, nobody was going to catch me. I just set off aimlessly as soon as the ball hit the back of the net, triggering a huge explosion of noise as it did so. I just felt an urge to sprint. Glenn tried to grab me but I wriggled free. Then I dodged past Steve Archibald. I was evading my own teammates just as I'd evaded my opponents moments earlier. How could I describe that sensation? It's almost impossible to find the words. For a spell of maybe five or ten seconds it was more thrilling than anything else I've ever experienced in my life. I went cold with excitement. It was utterly exhilarating.

John Motson: *"Ricky Villa has scored twice in this replay, having been taken off on Saturday . . . the tears have turned to triumph for him . . . and Spurs have got 12 minutes to hold out."*

We did hold out, and the FA Cup was ours. I'm not a

selfish man, but my first thought was for myself. When I moved to England in 1978 it was such a risk – for both parties – and I had such a difficult time adapting to life abroad. Then I'd stepped onto the big stage for the Cup final and fluffed my lines. But all that stress and strain seemed to disappear in a flash. A single, magical moment. With one mazy run it was as though my switch to Tottenham had been vindicated. It had all been worthwhile. I knew that whatever else happened from that point on, I'd made my mark on the history of a great club. It was like saying a big thank you to Keith Burkinshaw, for his patience and unyielding faith, and to all the Tottenham supporters for the incredibly warm welcome they afforded me and my family. I'd given something back, a lasting memory to cherish.

It was total redemption. The dejection I'd felt just five days before was consigned to the past. The despair of letting my family down, that overwhelming sense of regret, was all forgotten. Little more than a year earlier I'd been advised to quit the game. Then I went into the FA Cup final fearing it would be my last game for Tottenham. One match-winning performance later and my future was suddenly looking a lot brighter. Life was good again.

As for my good friend Garth, he was speaking to my eldest daughter Maru not so long ago. He told her that he was not happy with me. "I scored twice in an FA Cup semi-final, and once in an FA Cup final," he explained. "But your father went and scored great goals in both games. He totally upstaged me. Nobody remembers my goals. And it's all your father's fault." Sorry Garth. But it's all about picking your moments!

The formalities flashed by in a blur. Walking up the famous steps. Stevie lifting the trophy. Receiving our medals. The lap of honour. The photographers. So many photographers. Supporters threw us scarves and hats to wear while we skipped around the pitch parading the cup. It was pure joy. Pandemonium is the only word I could use to describe the state of our dressing room after the game. It was so busy. The room was full of people – deliriously happy people – while champagne was being sprayed all over the place. Everyone was singing *Ossie's Dream* and the man himself dented the cup by dropping it next to the team bath. The two of us were whisked away to a studio for a live interview to Argentina. From there we headed back to White Hart Lane and into the Chanticleer, a bar at the ground where we celebrated all through the night. I eventually got into bed at around 6 am, completely exhausted both physically and emotionally. I don't remember much about that party. But I do remember that I scored at Wembley to win the FA Cup, and that my life was never the same again.

Chapter Fourteen
LAS MALVINAS

Winning the FA Cup in 1981 confirmed Tottenham's re-emergence as a major force in English football. That Wembley triumph against Manchester City projected the club back up the ranks, restoring its status as one of the game's big players. The capture of another trophy in 1982 – again, the FA Cup – further enhanced our reputation as a leading side. That year had promised to be even more fruitful though; for long spells of the 1981/82 season we were serious contenders on four fronts.

From a personal point of view, my career-defining exploits at Wembley prompted a complete turnaround in fortunes. There's nothing quite like scoring the winning goal in an FA Cup final to remind a club of your worth. One glorious performance seemed to do precisely that, judging by the new two-year contract I was handed soon after. Unlike the terms I'd been offered before the final, the revised deal was most acceptable. With my immediate future secured I went back to Argentina for the summer where I slipped straight back into my natural routine, visiting the family ranch, riding horses, shooting and enjoying plenty of barbeques. And, of course, we talked about *that* goal. Everyone wanted to talk about it. All the people in my town had watched it on television so it was a popular conversation starter. I was more than happy to field their questions on the subject.

Back at base Keith made a significant addition to the squad by signing Ray Clemence, the England goalkeeper, who joined us from Liverpool, while defender Paul Price arrived from Luton Town. Apart from that, the team remained the same. The younger players, both those who had been developed by the club (Falco, Hazard, Hughton, Miller and Brooke) and those drafted in from non-league football (Roberts and Galvin), were one year more experienced. More importantly, we began the campaign brimming with confidence, having just landed some major silverware. We had discovered a winning mentality.

That 1981/82 campaign was undoubtedly my best as a Tottenham player. I discovered a confidence that had eluded me for much of the previous three years. I finally felt like a core member of the team, not just a fringe player constantly trying to prove himself. My Cup final performance seemed to change the way I was treated by the rest of the Spurs side too. In playing terms that is. Before the final I would drop deep to receive the ball but didn't always get it. After the Cup final it was different. My teammates were willing to pass me the ball, even in tight situations. They trusted me more. I scored nine goals that term, including three in a 6-1 victory over Wolves at White Hart Lane, as Spurs fans finally began to see the best of me on a more consistent basis.

Sadly, we just didn't possess the strength in depth to cope with the demands of that season. In a way, we were the victims of our own success. By reaching the League Cup final (where we lost to Liverpool, 3-1 after extra time), the FA Cup final (where we beat QPR, after a replay) and the European Cup Winners' Cup semi-finals (where we lost to Barcelona) our title challenge suffered. We were genuine contenders for most of the campaign, but all those Cup games led to a series of injuries and a huge backlog of fixtures. Our first XI was a tremendous side. What we didn't have, though, was quite the same quality in reserve, or the necessary consistency to become champions. Our potential for scoring goals was huge, which meant that on our day we could beat anyone. We lost too many silly games though, and it was our inability to consistently overcome teams lower down the table that ultimately cost us.

Liverpool won the championship that season, as they did in all but one of my years as a Spurs player. They almost always got the better of us, although we did come within a couple of minutes of beating them in the League Cup final that season. I never felt as though a psychological barrier existed when it came to facing Liverpool, I just think they were an extremely tough team to beat.

A more telling factor in the collapse of our title charge that year was that late pile-up of games. The English league must be one of – if not *the* – hardest championships to win. Contesting your final eight games in the space of just 17 days as we did in 1981/82, playing on Saturday–Monday–Wednesday–Saturday and so on, makes it virtually impossible. Due to the physical demands of that run we had no option but to spend the day after each match lying on the sofa. We had to rest. Then the day after that we would be playing again. Players were going into games less than 100 per cent fit, and tiredness was fundamental to our failure that year. The dynamic nature of English football – not to mention the fact that teams were only allowed to use one substitute in those days – only made it harder for us to cope. *And* we had to make do without our star man during that spell: Ossie, who left us well before the end of that season to attend Argentina's World Cup training camp, was among the best players around at that time. We eventually finished in fourth place.

Losing to Barcelona in the Cup Winners' Cup that year was a particularly bitter experience. That Barcelona team was as far removed from the side currently representing the Nou Camp giants as you could possibly imagine. I know I'm not alone in admitting that Barcelona are my favourite team to watch right now. For me, Pep Guardiola has got it spot on. His side play the way football should be played. Not so the team of '82. They were outrageously cynical. Barcelona were not only violent, but also difficult to break down, because they sat back with so many men behind the ball. We drew 1-1 at White Hart Lane and lost 1-0 in Spain. Sadly, it was not unusual for Spanish teams to adopt such an approach at that time. Juan Carlos Touriño, for example, was an excellent defender who joined Real Madrid from my old club Quilmes in 1970. He was a cultured, technical player. On arriving at the Bernabeu, however, he was told, "Keep playing your football . . . but you must also kick the opposition." Physical intimidation was encouraged.

While that campaign of 1981/82 presented me with a series of tough encounters as a footballer, the challenge I was posed off the pitch towards the end of that season – one I could never have envisaged – was testing on a vastly different scale. At the beginning of April 1982, as Tottenham prepared to take on Leicester City in an FA Cup semi-final at Villa Park, Argentinian troops invaded the Falkland Islands. Situated a few hundred miles off the southern tip of Argentina, *las Malvinas* – as they are known in South America – had been a source of friction ever since the British had claimed control there about 150 years earlier. For patriotic Argentinians, the Falklands – which we feel belong to us – held great symbolic importance. Since long before 1982, children in Argentina had been taught about the history of the islands at school.

By 1982, the popularity of Argentina's brutal ruling military junta was waning massively, due to continuing human rights violations and the country's chronic economic problems. In a desperate bid to boost their standing among the public, the regime, led by General Leopoldo Galtieri, decided they would reclaim the Falklands. It was a typically bungled operation. Galtieri's notion that Britain would allow the invasion to pass without a military response was hopelessly misplaced. Britain did respond, taking on and defeating Argentina's ill-trained and ill-equipped forces.

The Falklands War put us in an extremely awkward situation. Ossie had long been scheduled to leave the country anyway, regardless of the conflict, because he was joining up with Argentina's World Cup squad straight after our semi-final against Leicester (a 2-0 victory in which I didn't play; Ossie did, and received passionate backing from Tottenham supporters, and a chorus of boos from opposing fans). I wasn't in the World Cup squad so I decided to stay at Spurs. As you can imagine, I didn't feel comfortable. My home country and my adopted country were at war. It was awful.

Throughout it all, Tottenham handled the situation brilliantly. Nothing was too much for them to make us feel at ease. As for my teammates at Spurs, they made it immediately clear that the hostilities would have no effect at all on the friendship that I enjoyed with each of them. They just said, "This is not a problem between me and you, Ricky, it's a conflict between governments a long way away." They were totally understanding, which was typical. From the moment I first walked through the gates at White Hart Lane I'd been treated impeccably, so the club's considerate take on the situation didn't surprise me.

The incident completely dominated the national news, and generated interest all over the country. I have to say, the English public were very fair to us during this period. In my opinion, the fact that Britain has had many conflicts in the past means the people are more used to this type of situation, a little more accepting of it perhaps. A different mentality exists in Argentina, though, when it comes to the subject of war. I discovered this at first hand via a telephone interview I conducted with Bernardo Neustadt, a famous TV and radio broadcaster in Argentina. I agreed to take his call at 6 am English time, and I gave him my honest assessment of the situation. I said that I didn't agree with any war because the loss of so many lives is a tragedy, and that I hoped things could be resolved in other, more civilised ways. Neustadt, who supported Galtieri and his decision to invade, took offence at my stance. He'd wanted me to bad-mouth the English, to declare my approval of the war and effectively pledge my allegiance to the military government. Because he didn't like what I said he cut me off, finishing the conversation by saying, "If you ever decide to come back to Argentina, we will forgive you." He was implying that I was some kind of traitor. I'll never forget that. I made an effort to get up early and accept his call. I thought the war was stupid, a pointless exercise, and I told him that. He was rude to me, extremely unfair.

That episode, which gives an indication of the mood in Argentina at the time and also illustrates the divisive nature of war, left me feeling really angry.

While I received a hostile response when expressing my opinion back home, the treatment we were afforded by the people of England was completely respectful. In May 1982, one month into the War, our second daughter, Martina, was born. Because it was at its height, Cristina was placed in a separate room in the hospital in Hertford and not on the general ward – as a precautionary measure just in case anyone decided to do anything crazy. We needn't have worried. Never did anyone threaten us in England. On the contrary, we received so many congratulatory cards and flowers from local people. Some of the cards contained messages saying "Sorry for what's happening". It was amazing. Those gestures were unbelievable. Just recently I was in Hertford when a man approached me. "Ricky Villa!" he exclaimed, before announcing that he was a big Spurs fan. He then said, "I've got a son called Ricky. He was named after you because he was born at the same time as your daughter, in the same hospital." I gave him a big hug!

Martina, incidentally, wasn't actually born in the hospital. She was taken there straight after the birth. In keeping with the madness that surrounded the arrival of our first daughter Maru – when our 'chauffeur' Ossie got lost on the way to the hospital – Martina's big entrance also had a touch of farce about it. I was present for the birth of Maru, but not Martina. It was a Tuesday evening and I was in Nottingham with the rest of team, preparing for a meeting with Forest the following night.

Because the process of giving birth to Maru had been so

prolonged Cristina decided to remain at our house in Turnford for as long as possible before going to hospital. That was the plan, anyway. She was accompanied by her parents, who had flown over to stay with us, so was in good hands. Cristina was relaxing in a hot bath when her contractions started. With the help of her mother she just about managed to get out of the bath, got dressed and made her way downstairs. It soon became clear that time was against them though. It was too late to make a dash for the hospital. The only option was to phone our local GP, Dr Mukherjee – a close friend of ours to this day – who responded to the emergency call by rushing to our house armed with her medical bag. Dr Mukherjee examined Cristina before announcing, "It's on the way!" Cristina's mother frantically scampered off to fetch a towel and all those present prepared for the birth.

By this time, our great friends and neighbours Franco and Asunta had also been roped in to help out. When I phoned home from the serene setting of our team hotel at around half past eight in the evening I had no idea of the chaos that was unfolding at the other end of the line. Cristina was in the lounge, lying on the sofa in obvious discomfort as she was about to give birth, aided by the doctor and supported by her mother as well as Asunta. I was being given a live commentary over the phone by Franco in a loud mixture of Italian and broken English while Cristina's father was looking after two-year-old Maru in the garden. Even our little pet rabbit had a role to play, helping to distract Maru from the main event.

Italians are, by nature, emotional, passionate people, and Franco is no different. In this instance, he could hardly contain himself. "It's coming, it's coming! The baby's coming!" he yelled. I could only imagine how Cristina must have been feeling, but I do know it was pure agony for me. "I can see the head!" screamed Franco from his position across the room. "What are you talking about?" shouted a fraught Cristina. "You can't see anything from over there." Franco was getting a little carried away. "Yes! Now I see it!" he shrieked. "Really Franco?" I enquired. "Er . . . hang on a minute," he replied. Eventually Martina was born, on our sofa, on 11th May 1982. I was exhausted! Keith asked me if I was OK to play against Nottingham Forest and I said, "Yes. No problem. Why not?" I played against Forest the following night, and then returned home to meet my new daughter for the first time.

Martina's arrival provided us with a rare moment of joy in an otherwise stressful period. On a professional level, the saddest consequence of the Falklands War for me was missing out on playing in another FA Cup final. The decision not to consider me for the 1982 final against QPR was made following a discussion between Keith and myself. As much as it disappointed me, I just didn't think it would be right for me to appear in the match. Tottenham had received letters from relations of those who had been killed during the conflict, and with the War at the forefront of everyone's thoughts it was such a sensitive issue. The FA Cup final is a truly English occasion, and for me to have participated in it while my country was at war with England would have been wrong. I didn't want to play under those circumstances. The decision to omit me was a logical one.

I stayed away from Wembley on Cup final day, opting to remain at home instead. We weren't alone though, as five or six reporters and press photographers camped outside the house from about ten o'clock in the morning until six in the evening. It was a little unnerving, so I called the police. They said they were unable to act because our 'visitors' were in a public place and weren't actually bothering us. Tottenham sent a security guard along and I stayed indoors – I didn't dare step outside – peeping through the curtains every now and then to see if the group had dispersed. "How long are they going to hang around here for?" I kept wondering. Apart from that day, however, I didn't feel as though I was being hounded by the press.

The final was drawn 1-1 and, just like 12 months earlier, a replay was required to determine the winner. This time I did attend. It was quite a brave move really, but I donned my suit and sat behind Keith on the bench. I wanted to support the boys, and as I walked to my seat the Spurs fans sung my name. Coming at such a difficult time as it did, it was a gesture that genuinely moved me. It was a strange, emotional evening. One year earlier I had been the hero, the toast of Wembley. Now I was still part of the team but, as I watched from the sidelines, I had no control over the match. I was full of uncertainty. Had I played my last game for Tottenham? Would I ever hear the Spurs supporters sing my name again? As for my conduct that night, I was in a bit of an awkward situation. It goes without saying that I wanted us to win. But I knew that if we beat QPR then it may have been deemed inappropriate behaviour to the people of Argentina if I was seen to be celebrating and enjoying the occasion. Eventually we did win, with Glenn scoring the only goal of the game from the penalty spot. A long, hard season had taken its toll on us – we just about hung on to retain the trophy – but at least we finished a thrilling campaign with some kind of reward, even if it had at times promised to yield so much more.

After the Cup final I went back to Argentina for a few weeks. When I got there I couldn't believe what I was hearing. I sat with my family and friends, and naturally the main topic of conversation was the War. Due to the military regime's outrageous propaganda machine, though, people in Argentina were convinced our country was winning. "We're going to keep *las Malvinas*," they said. "Yesterday we killed 600 Brits in the Battle of Goose Green." I said "Are you sure? I don't think that's true. I didn't read anything like that in the English newspapers." I was accused of being brainwashed by the English. I said to Cristina, "I hope to God we're not wrong here, because if we are we'll have to leave Argentina. People will think we're supporting the English. Even our friends might shun us."

The ruling junta controlled all sources of information in Argentina – TV, radio, newspapers and magazines. They were lying to disguise their own failings, and in doing so whipped up the public into a false state of hysteria. The people had been turned so emphatically against Britain and were so sure that Argentina was on the verge of an historic triumph. I read reports of people being interviewed on the streets of Buenos Aires – members of the public, such as taxi drivers – and they were declaring, "We're going to beat the English!" The Argentinian press would claim that 600 British soldiers had been killed, while British papers on the same day would report the loss of just ten. The style of such reports in the UK was extremely formal, listing the name, rank and age of the deceased, and there was no doubt in my mind as to which one was the more accurate. I can't emphasise enough the madness of the situation in Argentina during this period. I remember in Roque Pérez there was a collection to raise money for the War effort. People donated money, jewellery, and even brand new motorbikes. It was crazy. I have absolutely no doubt that all that money and all those possessions would have been pocketed by various members of the junta.

Significantly, Pope John Paul II visited Argentina and urged the matter to be settled. He asked for Argentina to make an honourable surrender and eventually that's what they did, on June 14th, after 74 days of conflict. The Argentinian people were stunned. Completely disillusioned. One day they thought they were winning the War, and the next they realised it had all been a big charade. They wondered what on earth was going on. Part of me was relieved to have been proved correct, although in no way was I satisfied. We all know now that the approach of the Argentinian military was flawed. They fought in the wrong places and their tactics were botched. The USA and Chile assisted Britain, but the main reason that Argentina lost the Falklands War was their own incompetence. If there was anything positive to come out of the whole sorry episode then it was the change of rule it brought about. Thankfully, in 1983, the military's reign came to an end, and democracy returned to Argentina.

I saw the War from both sides. It was a difficult time for me and my family. All in all I'm happy with my behaviour during it. I had a clear conscience then and I have a clear conscience now. I never wished to express a strong opinion for either side. In my view, because of their close proximity to my country, the Falklands should belong to Argentina. I don't see why we shouldn't strive to reclaim the islands – diplomatically that is, not through fighting. I most definitely did not agree with the military regime that instigated the conflict as a last-ditch attempt to retain power.

I returned to Spurs for the 1982/83 season, but for the first time since joining the club I began the campaign as the only South American on the playing staff. Ossie felt really low that summer – the War affected him quite badly. He decided the time wasn't right to go back to England and instead joined Paris St Germain, in a proposed year-long loan arrangement, to stay out of the spotlight. I only found out about it when I came back from my holidays. It was hard to maintain contact in those days and I didn't know where he'd gone at first. Without wishing to sound too soppy, I did miss Ossie. I felt a bit lonely, I suppose. When I finally got the chance to speak to him, he told me that Paris wasn't what he'd expected. I could sense that he was unhappy there. Keith loved Ossie – just last year when I met him at a function the first thing he asked was "Where's Ossie?" – and towards the end of 1982 Spurs and PSG came to an agreement. Ossie resumed his Tottenham career the following January. I was delighted to have him back.

That passage of time was all a bit strange really – the War, the missed FA Cup final, Ossie's temporary absence. As was to be expected, there was a degree of resentment directed my way in the season that followed the Falklands conflict. There were some away games in which I was booed and insulted, although other sections would sometimes counter that with a show of support. It wasn't that bad really. Can you imagine if an Englishman had been playing football in Argentina at that time? It would have been impossible to survive. Besides, I could understand the anger of the few who did hurl insults. People lost loved ones in the War, so I reasoned that if they wanted to boo me then that was perfectly acceptable.

Nowadays when I'm back in England chatting amongst

people at a function, invariably the subject of the Falklands War comes up. Time has of course eased a lot of tension surrounding the issue. I was talking to some English guys at a recent social event, for example. They were smiling, saying "We were there first – the Falklands are ours!" And I said, "Yes, but you are more than 10,000 kilometres away – they're right on our doorstep!" Everyone laughed. We can discuss it in that manner now, without any aggression or animosity. The seriousness of that conflict will never be lost on me. It affected thousands of people – including myself – but is now in the past, where it belongs. We have to get on with our lives.

Chapter Fifteen
STARS, STRIPES AND SUNSHINE

J oining Tottenham had represented a huge gamble for all parties concerned. But fortune favours the brave, as they say, and I believe that – having each taken a calculated risk – Tottenham, myself and Ossie all got lucky. We found ourselves at a club that treated us perfectly, as players and also as human beings. They could not possibly have done any more for us. At the same time, I think that Keith Burkinshaw got lucky too. He'd seen us play at the World Cup, but he couldn't be sure of the type of characters on whom he'd taken such an expensive risk. What he soon found out was that his new recruits were proud professionals, committed, personable, family-orientated and trustworthy. Not like many other Argentinian players from that era, it has to be said, who were rebellious, ill-disciplined and irresponsible.

I take great pride in the fact that the two of us left a positive impression of Argentinian people. I believe that our efforts opened the door for other players from my country to follow a similar career path themselves in later years. We also demonstrated that it was possible to adapt to foreign surroundings, at a time when moving abroad as a footballer was virtually unheard of. The whole experience of living and playing in England was a fantastic period in my life. Like all good things, though, it came to an end. Do I regret leaving Tottenham? Absolutely. In the summer of 1983, after five seasons as a Spurs player, I was out of contract. When I joined the club my initial deal was for three years, and after winning the FA Cup in 1981 I signed for a further two. With that deal expiring I had a big decision ahead of me. In retrospect, I chose badly.

The first mistake I made was in misreading Keith's evaluation of me as a player. I was under the impression that he was happy to let me go. In English football you had to prove yourself every day, whether it be in training or a competitive match situation. All the time you were expected to perform. As I've already admitted, I struggled to operate at that intensity. I didn't always give 100 per cent in training and I thought that Keith frowned upon that. Keith used to stress the importance of having a good attitude in terms of working hard and fighting for every ball. Those were never my principal attributes. That physical element was the least motivational side of football for me. If I was asked to run five or six kilometres I'd think, "No thanks". With a ball at my feet though, I would run all day long.

I've since discussed the issue of my departure from Spurs with Keith and I would appear to have got it wrong. He didn't really want to get rid of me. I'm closer to Keith now than when I was playing under his managership. It wasn't like we didn't get on back then, we just never really connected. I always felt that Keith wasn't entirely happy with me. An example of the type of incident that led me to make that assumption occurred before an away game in my first or second season at Spurs. I can't remember exactly whom we were playing, West Bromwich Albion maybe. What I do recall is that we were in a bit of a rut. We were finding it difficult to take control of matches, and defensively we were too fragile. In an attempt to resolve the situation Keith sat down with me, Ossie and Glenn the day before the game. He was sure he'd identified a problem area. "We're not fighting hard enough in midfield," he said. "I'm thinking of changing things in there." He then asked each one of us, "How do you feel?" Glenn said "Perfect, really good." He turned to Ossie. "Great," he replied. Then it was my turn to answer. I hesitated a little – such is my nature – shrugged my shoulders and said "I feel . . . OK." The next day I was left out and John Pratt played instead.

I would say we had three 'untouchables' at Tottenham. Three players, that is, who were Keith's favourites, his generals out on the pitch: Ossie, Glenn and Stevie P. It doesn't take a great deal of thought or analysis to work out why. They were exceptional players. I was never part of that elite set, but for that I can only blame myself. My inconsistency saw to that. My relationship with Keith is far more relaxed now. More natural. In previous years I would just say hello to him, we would exchange pleasantries and make small talk. It's different now. We're not work associates any more, we're friends. A little while ago Keith was in Argentina – I think the visit was related to his role as assistant manager at Watford – and he came to my house in Roque Pérez for a barbeque. It was a wonderful day. We had a good laugh. I jumped at the opportunity of inviting him into my home. He was able to see how I lived, he saw my town and met my family. He saw me in my natural habitat. I don't think that Keith had ever *really* known me up to that point. In fact, it was difficult for English people in general to fully familiarise themselves with my personality because of the difficulties I encountered with the language. That was my fault of course. I'm just glad that Keith was able to make that journey. We understand each other now. We really get along well, even if "Where's Ossie?" is still the first question he asks me whenever I see him!

When it came to making the move away from White Hart Lane there were a few factors involved. I'd got to a point where I was tired of the weather, and I had this idea of playing in America. It's funny when I look back at my life and consider certain moments that left a lasting impression on me, particularly as an innocent youth. When I was about 18 years old I played for the Argentina under-20s in Peru. I remember sitting in the airport in Lima and looking up at the information board. I was instantly drawn to the name Miami. It fascinated me. The people who were making their way to that departure gate were so stylish, so elegantly dressed and good-looking. Miami seemed such an exotic destination to a teenager from the simple surroundings of Roque Pérez. I was mesmerised, and that's where my desire to play in America was rooted. That dreamy ambition to experience for myself the delights of Florida never left me. In addition to that, each season in the NASL (the North American Soccer League) was only six months long, which meant I could spend the rest of the year in Argentina. I asked Glenn Hoddle's agent Dennis Roach to find me a club and he arranged a deal with the Fort Lauderdale Strikers. Almost 15 years after first aspiring to get a taste of life in the Sunshine State I was off to make a new start in Florida with Cristina and our two little girls. I was excited by the prospect of a fresh challenge in a fresh environment.

Tottenham didn't make much of an effort to keep me. I must admit, I thought they might try to talk me out of it. But they didn't. I told them I was off to America and they let me go. Five years after striding through the front gates of White Hart Lane amid a flurry of publicity, I slipped out through the back door virtually unnoticed. Leaving Spurs was a huge error. I left a great league for an inferior one, and a significantly inferior one at that. But you have to live with your decisions. I can't go back and change it.

I wouldn't say that playing in the States was a waste of time. Certainly not. There were plenty of positives to take from the experience. First of all, Florida was a beautiful place to live. We were in Pompano Beach, which is just north of Fort Lauderdale, right next to the sea. We enjoyed a fantastic lifestyle. Some of the features of the area were like nothing I'd ever seen before. I would often discover things that were completely new to me. Like the moveable bridges in Miami. I'd be driving through the city when I would stop at a red light, which may not sound like an out-of-the-ordinary experience. But it was in Miami. I would sit and watch as the each side of the bridge was raised up and a magnificent ship would sail through. It was like being on a movie set. I'd only ever seen stuff like that in films. There were several of these bridges, placed about ten streets apart, and it all added to the attraction of the area.

Another perk of playing for Fort Lauderdale was the opportunity to speak my native language. Not so much when I was with the team, although the physical trainer was Puerto Rican and our best player was the Peruvian legend Teófilo Cubillas, so we conversed in Spanish. But there was a large Latin community in what was a very multicultural area, which meant that I could communicate naturally with most people. The language barrier that had caused me so much anguish in England didn't really exist in Florida. On top of all that our children were happy there, so it certainly wasn't a miserable period for us.

As for my game, I must say that it really improved during my time with Fort Lauderdale. I became a much better player. A much better tennis player that is. I must have played every single day. Because it was so hot in Florida the football team trained from about seven o'clock in the morning until 9:30 am. My family would still be sleeping when I got home from work. The rest of the days were our own, and that's when I really learned how to play tennis. There were courts at our condominium where I would play against local boys of around 15–16 years of age who were aspiring to become professional players. They had dreams of claiming big rewards on the tennis circuit but at that time they had to make do with the $10 I offered them each day to face me. Those kids were excellent technical players and I was no Björn Borg. They were far more stylish than me. But as a professional footballer I was in good physical condition, which compensated for my lack of finesse. I was more powerful than my opponents, naturally, which enabled me to win most of the matches. Tennis is a fantastic game. I still play now, and follow all the major events on television.

As for the football . . . that wasn't such a fulfilling experience. Playing football in the USA wasn't like playing football anywhere else. The standard was poor for a start. I would say it was roughly equivalent to the Third Division in England. The marquee names that had been lured to launch the NASL in the 1970s – the likes of Franz Beckenbauer, Johan Cruyff, Pelé, Bobby Moore and George Best – had all gone by the time I arrived, leaving a significant void in terms of the league's quality.

It wasn't just the moderate performance levels that were a problem, though. The situation went beyond that. The States has no real history of football, or 'soccer' as they prefer to call it. Football there was a very light concept. Baseball, basketball, ice hockey and American football are all sports that are deeply ingrained in their culture. But not football as we know it. I was used to playing in such an intense, competitive environment in Argentina and then England, where football means so much to the people. There everyone looks forward to the weekend, because that's when their team is playing. Each result determines the supporters' mood for the rest of that day, or week or even longer. People in Argentina and England are crazy about football. The game is everywhere – on television and the radio, in newspapers and magazines. In every bar, factory or office, and on every street corner, the topic of conversation will soon come round to football. It's an obsession. Going from that environment to the more serene surroundings of America's NASL was really difficult. A big culture shock.

One day I was chatting with an American guy near my condominium. I told him that I was a footballer and he told me that he wasn't really a fan of the game. He asked me, "Why do people get so excited about soccer? What's so good about it?" What's so good about football?! Where do I start? I thought that if this man didn't understand what was beautiful about football – even if he was only vaguely familiar with the game – then there was no point in me trying to explain. He just didn't get it. And that seemed to be the case with so many Americans.

Watching football in America at that time was more of a social gathering more than anything else. There was as much entertainment outside the ground as there was in it. Fans were enticed to the stadium a couple of hours before kick-off by a sort of fairground next to the arena, with customary rides for the children and an assortment of other fun attractions. There were barbeques and beer tents. Free T-shirts and mini footballs were also on offer, all acting as incentives to draw the people in. What you got as a result was not really a football crowd in the traditional sense. Some pockets of fans would sporadically burst into song, and in places like San Jose, Vancouver and Chicago the games attracted a bigger audience of up to 15,000 or so. But in general the atmosphere in each stadium was all very innocent and reserved.

Football in the USA has progressed remarkably since I played there. The MLS is an established league that has attracted the likes of David Beckham in recent years, while the national team's regular presence at the World Cup means that America can no longer be dismissed as a nation with little interest in football. But back in the 1980s it was different. The NASL was full of surprises for me. Essentially, they didn't really grasp the fundamentals of the game. It was all about the statistics over there. Statistics, statistics, statistics. The Americans are obsessed with them. They analyse their sports in such detail, with a vast range of data emanating from every game. Be it batting averages in baseball, blocks and rebounds in basketball or interceptions in the NFL, a series of numbers are used to evaluate each player's performance. The same level of scrutiny was applied to football. Making the pass or cross that directly preceded a goal – the coveted 'assist' – was deemed virtually as important as scoring the goal. In any country that is serious about football it is easy to access a simple chart detailing the national league's leading goalscorers. In America though, nothing is that simple when it comes to statistics. The NASL produced a more elaborate index to rate the players. Two points were awarded for scoring a goal, one for providing the assist. Even the pass *before* the assist – whatever that was called – was regarded as a notable action.

There was great importance attached to this performance index. It was everyone's first point of reference when evaluating a player's display. How did Ricky Villa perform? Check the statistics. That was the mentality and it wasn't really appropriate. All the players were judged by their data. When a club was preparing to add to the playing staff the first thing that coaches and directors did was to consult the statistics. They couldn't do without it. It was such a misleading system, though. A player could look good on paper in terms of his numbers but that certainly didn't guarantee that he was a decent footballer. The rating index affected the way that many individuals approached the game. For instance, there were no points on offer for defending so everyone poured forward in search of enhancing their personal tallies. It was crazy! Players were so obsessed with claiming an assist they would often make the wrong decisions at crucial moments. This was a completely foreign way of thinking for me. I could never quite get my head around it. I wasn't a selfish player. My objective was to help the team.

One player in the Fort Lauderdale side who didn't need a positive statistical profile to prove his worth was Cubillas. A simple set of numbers could never do the man justice. He was an exceptional player. The World Cup in 1970 will forever be remembered for the wonderfully attacking Brazil side that won it, while eight years later Mario Kempes and the Argentina squad that I was proud to have been part of stole the show by lifting the trophy on home soil. In both those tournaments though, Peru's key man Cubillas was undoubtedly among the star performers. One of his goals, a free kick against Scotland that he bent around the wall with the outside of his right foot, features on almost every video collection of great World Cup strikes.

Cubillas was full of flair. Even though he was in his mid-30s and approaching the end of his playing career he was still a wonderful footballer. I loved playing alongside him. Sometimes in football you find yourself lining up on the same team as someone who shares precisely the same understanding of the game as you do. Call it instinctive, or even telepathic, but there are occasions when you instantly connect with a colleague. Not as a result of any specific work on the training field, or through discussing your intentions with that individual beforehand. Now and then, it is not necessary to make a concerted effort to forge an effective partnership with a teammate. It just clicks. That was the case with myself and Cubillas. We had a really natural understanding on the pitch, always on the same wavelength. We played a lot of one-twos, passing and moving our way around the opposition. He had the ability to resolve the most congested of situations on a football pitch. Ours was a combination rooted in South America of course, and one appreciated by many among the local Latin community who came to watch us play. The Fort Lauderdale supporters – of which roughly 10,000 would attend our home games – adored Cubillas.

Our main man was treated like a star, and rightly so. He was afforded the same luxuries as a number 10 in Argentina. "Don't fancy training today? No problem. Put your feet up." He had his own set of rules, but we knew he would perform come match day. As long as it was a home game that is, because he didn't always join us for away fixtures. I didn't object to that. He was too old to play every game, or train every day, and I was used to seeing a team give their pivotal players a little leeway in Argentina. There was a time when I was one of them in fact. Either way, it was an absolute pleasure to have linked up with one of the game's greats.

Not only did Cubillas defy his advancing years to justify a reputation as one of his generation's finest players, he did so on the most difficult of playing surfaces. The artificial pitches we played on in America were horrendous. I found it almost impossible to play on what were effectively worn-out synthetic carpets over there. Falling over was never a pleasant experience, while the hard ground meant that if the ball was allowed to bounce we would have to wait ages for it to come down again. Some drop kicks from the goalkeeper would leap off the surface and fly on for another 30 or 40 yards. I used to stand there in games watching the ball zooming backwards and forwards over my head wondering, "How am I supposed to control that?" It was horrible.

Another way in which I was regularly reminded how football differed in the NASL from almost anywhere else came on away trips. The routine that preceded those games in America was completely different from the build-up to matches in England. At Tottenham we would travel to a hotel the day before an away fixture and, as a team, we would meet for dinner that evening at around 8 o'clock. It was all very organised and professional. The team was firmly united on the pitch and that closeness stemmed from a tendency to stick together off the field of play too. That habit of spending time in each other's company breeds the team spirit that is crucial to the success of any side. It didn't work like that at Fort Lauderdale though. The pre-match procedure for away games was quite odd really. On arriving at our destination we were handed 25 dollars each to get ourselves something to eat. That was it. No group meal, no organised get-together, nothing. I found this extraordinary. The whole squad dispersed to various corners of the locality in search of food. Some of the lads would go off and get a burger, others would opt for pizza. We were not really close-knit as a group and this type of practice hardly helped foster camaraderie within the camp. It was a similar story after training, when everyone went their separate ways as soon as the session finished.

All in all, things didn't work out as I was hoping they would in the USA. Life in Florida itself was wonderful. That part of the experience definitely met my expectations. Living by the beach and waking up to sunshine every morning provided the perfect start to each day. The weather goes some way to dictating a person's mood. Life just feels better when the sun's out. This was the most positive aspect of swapping Spurs for the Strikers. I didn't really miss England's long grey winters, ploughing my way around the training pitch whilst ankle deep in mud. Or visiting Old Trafford in December and wondering where all the grass had gone.

The playing side of things Stateside was disappointing though. I was approaching my 31st birthday when I left Tottenham. I thought I would play for another two or three years and then retire; my plan was always to return home after that. So it seemed like the right time to make a move I'd long considered. To be honest, I'd lost the will to fight. Not just for a place in the Tottenham team, but the fight to maintain my reputation every single day. That was the situation in England. In every match and every training session I felt under pressure to perform to the very best of my ability. There was no breathing space, no let-up. My performance was constantly being assessed. I was ready to leave that high-pressure environment and start winding down my career I suppose. Florida seemed like an appropriate destination.

Despite signing a contract for two years when I joined the Strikers my American adventure was short-lived. Financially, the difference between playing for Tottenham and Fort Lauderdale was negligible. During the six-month season, that is. For the other half of the year my wages dropped by 50 per cent. That didn't bother me though. I went back home to Roque Pérez and was glad to be getting paid at all.

Whilst back in Argentina I was informed that Fort Lauderdale Strikers would be moving. Not just down the road or around the corner, but hundreds of miles inland to Minnesota. That kind of practice is almost unheard of in England and most other countries. But in America, where many teams are privately owned, it's fairly common for a club – or 'franchise' – to uproot and relocate. In this case, the Strikers were struggling economically in Florida. They were hiring the stadium and offices at a considerable cost and the owner had business interests in Minnesota. Transferring the team there seemed like a logical move to make. I wasn't interested in joining them though. I went to America to bask in the Florida sunshine, not the blizzards of Minnesota. I made my feelings known to the management. I signed for the Fort Lauderdale

Strikers, I told them, not the Minnesota Strikers. That wasn't part of the deal. Minnesota was too far away. Too cold. I used all the excuses I could think of to exclude myself from the relocation. I just wanted to stay at home. It took a fair degree of negotiating but, following a series of telephone exchanges, I eventually persuaded the Strikers to release me from my contract. I was a free man.

So at 31 years of age, and with plenty more football in me, I found myself without a club. My career had afforded me some incredibly uplifting moments. I'd been the most expensive player in my country's history. I'd seen a huge wave of joy sweep through Buenos Aires when the Argentina squad I was part of won the World Cup. I'd witnessed a nation's hysteria at first hand. I'd seen Wembley erupt when I scored a Cup final winner. I'd played in some of the biggest, noisiest, most famous arenas in the world. Now I was back home in my peaceful little town and things had all gone a bit quiet. What I did next still ranks among the proudest achievements of my career. But barely anyone outside of my local patch is aware of it.

Chapter Sixteen
LOCAL PRIDE

The Copa Vecar Varela is an amateur football tournament held in Argentina. Just as the FA Trophy is in England, it's the most prestigious prize on offer to those outside the full-time ranks. I actually won it with Atlético Tucumán in 1976/77, shortly before I left Atlético Tucumán for Racing Club of Buenos Aires. It may sound odd that I represented the province of Tucumán in an amateur tournament when I was on the verge of becoming the nation's costliest player. But the history of Argentinian football is littered· with such anomalies. Political interference, it has to be said, is no small factor in that.

I didn't want to play for Tucumán in the Copa Vecar Varela. I was a top-flight professional. I'd represented my country. Why should I take part in a competition that consisted mainly of part-timers? In the end I was given a perfectly good reason why I should play – because General Domingo Bussi said I should. General Bussi was the governor of Tucumán, installed by the military and feared by all. If he asked you to do something, like help the regional football team win a tournament that would in turn bring a little prestige to the area he ruled, then you did it. My initial objection to participating didn't go down too well among the local authorities. "So you don't fancy playing?" was their reaction. "Maybe you would like to talk to Mr Bussi about that?" A sudden change of heart was in order. I had no option but to partake, and General Bussi got his wish. We won the cup.

Seven years later I found myself competing for the Copa Vecar Varela title once again, only this time I needed no persuasion to participate. I came back to Roque Pérez following my US experience at the beginning of 1984. As a result of not returning to the now-Minnesota Strikers I went six or seven months without playing professionally, even though for much of that time I was still receiving a small salary from the US club. And it's not like I didn't make use of my spare time. I assisted my father around the farm and I played a bit of five-a-side football in the town to keep ticking over. I also arranged for a tennis court to be set up on our premises, to help satisfy a fierce passion for the game that I'd discovered in Florida.

In truth, I never really considered the potential consequences of this extended spell away from full-time football. Losing match sharpness wasn't really a concern. I just went with the flow, ruled by my heart rather than my head. Perhaps it wasn't the best action to take. But I didn't go without football completely. I went back to my roots: two decades after joining local team Santiago Larre as a 12-year-old boy I re-signed for them. I didn't rejoin my first ever club with the intention of playing for them, though. I did it in order to represent my home region of Roque Pérez in the Copa Vecar Varela, with competition rules stating that each player had to be affiliated to a team in the area. My official registration and accompanying documents were placed in the hands of little Santiago Larre.

So less than 12 months after leaving Tottenham I was playing for the Roque Pérez Select XI. Suddenly my team-mates had a distinctly less-renowned look about them. There was no Ardiles, Hoddle, Clemence or Archibald, never mind Kempes or Passarella, or that other World Cup great Cubillas. I had a new array of colleagues to familiarise myself with. Like right back Ruben Rato, who earned a living as a door-to-door salesman selling gas canisters and soda water. And striker *Gallegito* Garcia, who worked on a chicken farm. And goalkeeper Fernando Milani, who during the week could be found behind the counter of a local store.

We had a great run in the cup and I loved it. I didn't play in the early rounds but came into the team at the last-16 stage. As we progressed further in the competition we took it more seriously, training three nights a week and acquiring a physical trainer. Raffles and fund-raising events were held for the team, to cover the cost of travel and to pay the players a modest amount. Roque Pérez was gripped by the excitement of it all: a severe case of 'cup fever', as they say in England.

I was part of the Roque Pérez side that reached the Buenos Aires province final that year (four provincial winners across Argentina went on to contest the main trophy) and never before or since has a football team from my home region scaled such heights. It remains the town's finest football achievement. The locals still talk about it now. Temporary stands were erected to accommodate crowds of around 3,000 – half the town came to watch us play – and my brother-in-law Chacho has photographs from those games on the wall of his restaurant. My son Ricky still glances at those pictures, with a mass of terraced spectators in the background, and asks, "Where was this match played again?" I tell him it was right here in Roque Pérez and he gives me a puzzled look. He can't believe the local team ever attracted so much attention.

Even now I struggle to explain the thrill that came with representing my town. There were no major financial rewards on offer. And we were hardly competing for the world's most coveted honour. But none of that mattered. Representing the area I belonged to – the area that several generations of my family had belonged to – was uniquely fulfilling. To be surrounded by family and friends, all the people I'd grown up around, during such a memorable period was wonderful. We claimed a little piece of local history and that made me a proud man. Walking around the town was like 1981 all over again. Everyone was stopping me to wish me good luck and discuss the big game.

The final proved to be a step too far for us. Just getting to that stage was an astounding achievement really, considering the size of my town. Our opponents were Loma Negra, who represented the city of Olavarría. They took their name from the Loma Negra cement company that funded them, and with their hefty financial backing they were practically professional. We lost 6-0 at their place and then 1-0 at home. A proper stuffing. That first game in Olavarría gave a perfect example of the gulf in standing between the two teams. It was lashing down with rain but, as our sole professional, I was the only player in our side who had proper studs to wear. The Loma Negra team were all equipped with the appropriate footwear while our boys could hardly stand up. No wonder we were beaten so soundly.

Despite that defeat we took immense credit for our unlikely cup run. Roque Pérez is small in terms of land mass or population, but the town's passion for football is huge. I firmly believe that the local team could prosper at the fourth or fifth level of Argentine football. The network of support necessary to sustain a challenge at that standard definitely exists in the area. Thousands of people would attend the games.

For me personally, the cup exploits of Roque Pérez surprisingly revived my career. *El Gráfico* magazine did a feature along the lines of "Whatever happened to Ricky Villa?" after discovering that I was turning out for my local team. They interviewed me and thought it made a fantastic story. Up in the northern reaches of South America someone associated with Colombian outfit Deportivo Cali read the article. A representative of the club contacted me and asked if I would be interested in playing for them. Brief negotiations followed. I played in the second leg of the cup final for Roque Pérez against Loma Negra on a Sunday and on the Tuesday I flew to Colombia. Just like that, I was a professional footballer again.

Chapter Seventeen
END OF THE ROAD

Another day, another foreign excursion. I signed for Deportivo Cali halfway through 1984. They made me a decent offer, with a contract lasting until the end of 1985, and in truth they were the first club to express an interest after I returned home from America. It wasn't a difficult decision to make.

Life in Colombia afforded us another interesting experience. Cristina loved travelling. She enjoyed living in foreign countries, taking advantage of the opportunity to embrace different cultures. We were well looked after in Cali. We had a nice apartment with a swimming pool, and Maru began school in the city. We were happy there. I know that for many people the mere mention of Colombia conjures up thoughts of drugs and violence. It's true that drug barons enjoyed a long-standing association with Colombian football – owning a club provided a significant status boost, as well as a chance to launder money – and when I was in Cali there was talk of 'hot money' circulating within the sport. In addition, a series of high-profile incidents have blighted the game there. In the late 1980s the season was cancelled when a referee was assassinated, while – most famously – defender Andres Escobar was shot dead in 1994 shortly after scoring an own goal against the USA at the World Cup.

Personally, I never felt threatened in Colombia. Having said that, a considerable presence of security staff offered a constant reminder of the potential dangers. We were afforded round-the-clock protection at our complex, with four armed guards on patrol 24 hours a day. Even when Cristina went to the supermarket she would be followed by one of the guards. I saw a lot of guns in Colombia, and plenty of bodyguards too. The leading figures, such as the president, were always surrounded by a big group of heavies. I'd never witnessed security on that scale before. Sometimes we would hear reports of civil unrest in other parts of the country, but none of that stuff directly affected us. It was another different environment for us to experience, and one it didn't take too long to get used to. The Colombian people were nice and friendly. We were able to enjoy a pretty normal existence.

The strangest thing about Cali was that hardly any of the players had a car. At first I didn't either, so every morning I would hop on the bus – an old coach with a roof but no windows – that picked up all the players and took them to training. Can you imagine that? A whole squad of star foot-ballers hanging around on the street waiting to board a worn-out coach bound for training. The local lads didn't earn enough money to buy their own cars, but I soon bought one. No more bus trips for me.

Colombian football was characterised by a simple, positive style – beautiful football, if you like. Not cynical, or rugged. I played well for Deportivo. I didn't run around that much, but then I never did. This, I am sometimes reminded, is a source of much frustration for one of my old colleagues.

Whenever I bump into Américo Gallego, one of my World Cup-winning teammates, he says, "I used to run ten times as far as you in a game, so how come you're so thin and I'm so fat?"

On the subject of midfielders who were masters at conserving energy, I played alongside one of the best at Deportivo Cali. The young man's name was Carlos Valderrama. Two things were remarkable about Valderrama – his distinctive mop of blond hair and his outstanding natural ability. He was a special player. He was lazy, rarely broke sweat and never moved at anything quicker than jogging pace. Defending? Not for him. In fact, he hated defensive coaches, and succeeded in getting one or two of them fired. Just my type of player! What a creative force he was though. Everything went through him. He set the tempo – he could produce something from almost anywhere on the pitch – and was a genius in the final third. Valderrama was not the type to take on opponents, but was so precise with his passing that the balls he threaded inside defenders were impossible to cut out. It's no surprise that he went on to win more than 100 caps for Colombia and a South American Player of the Year title.

Valderrama was outstanding, although – in my opinion – he wasn't the best player in that Deportivo Cali team. That was Bernardo Redín, an attacking midfielder of less repute than Valderrama but certainly no less ability. Despite the efforts of Valderrama and Redín we struggled to get the better of our big city rivals América de Cali. They had some top players, like Argentine internationals Ricardo Gareca and Julio César Falcioni, and dominated Colombian football in the mid-1980s in much the same way as Liverpool did in England.

My time in Colombia finished on a sour note. I contracted

hepatitis B, a debilitating illness that left me feeling incredibly weak. I was told to stay in bed for a month, but tried to get up too soon and relapsed. As a result, I was bedridden for a total of four months. During this time the club stopped paying me so I confronted the Deportivo president. Because it was not advisable to start legal proceedings over there I lost out. In the end, I couldn't leave quickly enough. After 18 months in Colombia I left on bad terms which, unfortunately, is sometimes difficult to avoid when a player–club relationship comes to an end.

I recovered from that bout of hepatitis but, at 33 years of age, I was ready to retire from football. I went back to Argentina, where people were asking me if I'd quit. "Yes," I would reply. I thought that was it for me. It wasn't quite the end though. A very good friend of mine from my days as a Quilmes player, Hugo García, had moved into coaching. His team, the modest Buenos Aires club Defensa y Justicia, were about to start life in the second tier of Argentine football for the first time in their history. Hugo asked me to play for him and, at first, I declined the offer. He said, "Come on Ricky, this is a new level for us. We need a big name, someone with experience." Eventually he persuaded me to lace up my boots again. To begin with, he probably wished that he hadn't. I'd been out of the game for several months and only signed for the club one week before the season kicked off. My lack of training and match practice told – I was hopeless in my first six months as a Defensa player. It got to a stage where I sat down with Hugo and said, "I know we're friends but don't feel bad about putting me on the bench. Feel free to drop me." Hugo was having none of it. "You're a great player," he assured me. "You're staying in the team."

I did remain involved but – ironically I suppose – Hugo didn't. After winning promotion twice in quick succession Defensa had enjoyed a rapid rise up the divisions; inevitably perhaps, the team found it difficult initially to adapt to a new, elevated level. We spent the first half of that season near the foot of the table and Hugo was sacked, before a late-season revival saw us escape the drop. All things considered, just surviving has to go down as an achievement of sorts. Defensa is a modest club with modest resources, so to have held its own alongside much wealthier clubs took some doing.

After gradually rediscovering my rhythm that season I spent another two years with Defensa in the second tier. I was still playing in the No 10 position – albeit at a slower pace than before – and I still managed to score a few goals. Football became fun again. Defensa was a humble club, with an impressive collective spirit created by a group of fully committed, honest players. We played some decent, passing football. It was a bit like playing for Spurs in that respect, even to the point of losing games we really shouldn't have! Unfortunately I also had to deal with the more trying side of Argentinian football once again, with the late payment of wages a regular issue. As an elder statesman who had encountered identical problems as a youngster I assumed the role of peacemaker in these situations, making sure that all was calm in the camp. Despite the odd dispute there was a good feeling around the place.

I really enjoyed those years. I just wish I could have found my form a little earlier, and helped my companion keep his job. Hugo died in a car accident some years later. He was a good man and a good friend. I'll always be grateful to him for extending my playing career. You never quite appreciate it at the time, maybe because of the pressure and high expectations. But whichever path you follow once your playing career ends, attempting to find a similar thrill to the one that playing football provides is ultimately a futile pursuit.

Chapter Eighteen
TAKING CHARGE

At the age of 37 I played my last game as a professional footballer. I still got paid to play after that – $300 a game, for local side 25 de Mayo – but there was no training or full-time commitment involved. I also played for neighbouring town Lobos, by which time my role had evolved into that of a sitting midfielder. I really liked playing in that position – I could start moves from deep and, because holding midfielders are rarely man-marked, I enjoyed an unfamiliar sense of freedom. To begin with, I was completely comfortable with retirement. It felt like a good thing to me. A relief almost. You reach a point as a player when you realise you can't possibly go on, training every day and fighting for a place in the team. Always striving to meet expectations. In short, it was nice to have a break.

I didn't miss football at first. That feeling didn't last long, though. It soon became difficult, finding an alternative way of filling the great big void that quitting football had left in my life. I had to consider another way of earning a living. And, like so many retired footballers, that meant trying my hand at management. The first time I picked up the phone to hear someone asking me if I would like to manage their football club I said yes. Straight away, no hesitation. I wasn't even sure I wanted to be a football manager. I just needed something to concentrate on, some kind of purpose in life that had been missing since I'd stopped playing. Something to pass the time as much as anything else. I'd been involved in football all my working life, so why not try taking charge of a team? I'd played under some pretty good managers – some extremely good ones in fact – so I must have learned something. Even if I wasn't always paying attention during training. It seemed like a pretty natural move.

More than just filling a gap, management had an energising effect on me that I hadn't anticipated. I discovered a zest for the job. I was ambitious. At least, I was in my first managerial role. That first post as the boss was at Defensa y Justicia. I felt refreshed by my new occupation and was full of optimism. Blind, naive optimism perhaps, but optimism nonetheless. I convinced the players they were capable of achieving great things and, in turn, I felt as though they respected me. Following their relegation from Nacional B to *Primera B Metropolitana* in 1993 Defensa were playing in the third tier of Argentine football. I knew exactly how I wanted my team to perform. My vision was to implement a positive, attacking style of play and I was given free reign by the board to shape the team accordingly. I have to say it worked too. Under my guidance Defensa were something of a surprise package, playing an exciting brand of football that supporters still recall with great fondness. We lost out to Chacarita Juniors in the play-offs, but I felt the players improved and my stock as a manager was high. "I could get used to this management business," I thought. "There's nothing to it!" I was about to find out that it wasn't quite that simple.

It all started to turn sour soon after I parted company with Defensa. Having effectively served my apprenticeship there for a couple of years I'd developed a decent enough reputation. Even now, if there was one football club willing to trust me at the helm of their team it would be Defensa y Justicia. Recognising the relative success I'd achieved in my maiden venture as a manager, my old team Quilmes – then in the second tier and traditionally a bigger club than Defensa – came calling. My initial role there was that of general manager, with the overseeing of youth development one of my prime concerns. I was handed a lot more responsibility than I'd had at Defensa. When the Quilmes board decided to sack the first-team manager I was appointed in his place. As Quilmes was my first senior club as a teenager I've always retained a special affection for the place. Becoming manager there gave me an exciting opportunity to build my own team, with its own identity, at a club with which I had a genuine connection. I had aspirations of moulding that team in the expansive, offensive style of César Luis Menotti. Sadly, I couldn't make that happen.

There were a number of reasons for this. Interference from above was the main one, with the board making it difficult for me to succeed as manager of Quilmes. The president, for example, brought in players that he wanted at the club. As a result I found myself in charge of a team that had been forced upon me, as opposed to one that I'd assembled under my free will. I began to understand why Quilmes never seemed to grow as a club. There's no real progression, just constantly fluctuating fortunes: a promotion here and a relegation there. Economic problems ensure a yo-yo existence and I was left disillusioned by the whole experience. Hearing people on the local radio station being critical of myself and the team was also hard to digest. There was so much negativity. After just 11 games in charge I was shown the door.

At that stage I remained undeterred. Football clubs in Argentina change managers with greater frequency than in England. You just accept it and move on. I took over at another of the clubs I'd represented as a player, Atlético Tucumán. Again – big problems! I took over from Jorge *el Pipa* Higuaín, whose son Gonzalo spearheaded the Argentina attack at the World Cup in South Africa following an outstanding season with Real Madrid.

Atlético Tucumán sold me to Racing Club of Buenos Aires in the 1970s for a huge fee. They were a rich club back then. They weren't a rich club when I returned to manage them, though. The club was ravaged by in-fighting, with money the source of each conflict. I went three months without being paid. At times I found myself enveloped by darkness in my apartment because the electricity was cut due to the club's failure to pay the rent. No lights, no telephone. Every day was like a survival test. I tried to get the players their wages, although I sensed it was a case of each man for himself. I would talk to the players and then go to the board on behalf of the squad in a bid to arrange some kind of payment. I suspect the more experienced players went behind my back, though, attempting to negotiate their own individual deals with the directors. It all made for an unsettled camp.

Despite the testing conditions I was almost successful with Atlético Tucumán. Almost was not good enough, however. My Atlético team made the play-offs in 1996, with a top-flight place on offer for the series winner. In the semi-finals we were paired with Instituto of Córdoba, and after earning a creditable 1-1 draw away from home in the first leg we were optimistic of progressing to the final. For a club like Atlético Tucumán, with big ideas and ambitions, first division football is a must. We were on course to satisfy that demand when we led 1-0 in the return match. Then it all went wrong. We had a player needlessly sent off and the atmosphere inside the stadium changed immediately. It was like a cemetery. The team panicked, allowing Instituto to win 3-1 on the day and 4-2 on aggregate. That defeat marked the end of my stint as Atlético boss. I wasn't offered a new deal. I feel as though I was made a scapegoat, to be honest, taking the blame for the shortcomings of a badly run club where failure on the pitch stemmed from a debilitating level of incompetence further up the hierarchy. My desire to make it as a football manager was waning by the day.

I did have one more crack at management with Club Atlético Tigre, another second division club in Buenos Aires, where I was confronted with a whole new set of problems. Some of which were simply frightening. To begin with, the challenges I was presented with were not all that unusual to someone familiar with the ways of Argentine football. Off the pitch there were daily conflicts that revolved almost entirely around – you've guessed it – money. The players, as you would expect, just wanted to receive their wages but the club made excuses while they delayed making those payments. At any one time I would estimate that at least half the playing squad were unhappy. I sided with my players and inevitably clashed with directors. This type of financial wrangle was certainly nothing new. After I left Quilmes, for example, five or six years passed before I finally got paid the money they owed me.

On the playing side, I really struggled to reach the Tigre players. I was determined to stick to my principles. I envisaged my team adopting a neat, passing style of football. I wanted the supporters to be entertained. At Tigre I realised that not all players share that outlook. Argentina's Nacional B is a tough division. It's fast and furious, with most teams favouring the direct approach to goal. We had a fairly mediocre team at Tigre and many of the lads were set in their ways, preferring to whack the ball down the field rather than passing it ten yards and opting for a more patient build-up. Trying to change the players' mentality was tough. For me, long-ball football is low-risk football. If defenders are not comfortable with the responsibility that comes with possession of the ball their instinct is to kick it as far away from their goal as possible. They're scared to play for fear of losing possession and that goes for some managers too. Personally, I always urged my players to pass the ball.

So I failed to convince the playing staff of my footballing ideology while, at the same time, the board were not making life easy. The most alarming issues I encountered at Tigre, however, stretched beyond any dealings with players or directors. I was also confronted with an unnerving phenomenon that exists throughout the Argentine game.

The *Barras Bravas* are a prominent feature of Argentine football. Every club has a *barra brava* connected to it. Dating back several decades – to the 1950s or 1960s maybe – *barra brava* is a term used to describe an organised group of supporters. We're not talking about a regular fan club here, though; more a small-time criminal outfit, a sort of mafia. The *Barras Bravas* have a reputation for violence, but they're no ordinary hooligans. They have a significant influence on events at each club. It basically works as follows: club officials establish an association, or an understanding if you like, with the local *barra brava*. That *barra brava* controls club elections, by turning some people away at the polling station and pressurising others to vote for their man. They're also used to harass unwanted managers and players into quitting the club. In return, members of the *barra brava* are rewarded with match tickets and money.

I witnessed for myself exactly how the *Barras Bravas* operate when I was at Tigre. When we went to collect our wages – not in full, usually, and often late – the Tigre *barra brava* would line the corridors, having been tipped off by a contact inside the club that it was payday. We had to give them some of our money to effectively buy our own safety. It was crazy. These people knew precisely how much we were earning. They had a major influence at Tigre, which made it a dangerous club to manage. I've never felt so intimidated by the fans as I did at Tigre. The pressure was incredible. I remember when a member of the Tigre *barra brava* died in a car crash and all the staff were obliged to attend the funeral. You should have seen some of the faces on these people at the service. They had that look of delinquency. I had an urge to get away from there as fast as possible.

The most disturbing *barra brava*-related incident I can recall came during training one day. We used to train on a private ground, with security staff guarding the entrance. One morning we were in the middle of a session when a car came tearing across the field – having easily breached security – right up to the centre of the pitch. There were five guys in the car, although a couple of them were more out than in as they perched themselves on the window ledge of the car doors.

Their arrival brought training to a complete standstill. It was surreal, not to mention frightening – we didn't know if they were armed or not, or precisely what it was they planned to do. "We want to talk to you, Ricky Villa," they announced, after pulling up right beside me. I knew I had no choice but to entertain them. So we had a meeting. They didn't care for small talk. "We want to know if the players are following your orders," they said. "If not we will beat them up. Just tell us; we'll sort it out." I certainly wasn't about to betray my players. "It's fine," I said. "They're doing exactly as they're told." Our uninvited visitors then addressed the players who, thankfully, spoke of me in positive terms. Somehow, between us, we managed to appease the *barra brava* on that occasion.

When we lost 3-1 to local rivals San Miguel, however, I knew my time was up. That evening the Tigre president phoned me and said, "If you come to training on Monday I can't guarantee your safety. The *barra brava* is here at my house right now." That last bit may not have been true, but I got the message. I resigned immediately – after just 11 or 12 games at the helm – without so much as a chance to say goodbye to the players.

The *barra brava* phenomenon is an extreme example of how the conduct of football fans varies between Argentina and England. There are other differences that also illustrate this point. In Argentina, for instance, every defeat is met with fury by supporters. One bad performance and they cry, "Useless! . . . You're finished . . . See you later . . . Don't come back." In the eyes of the fans a player goes from a hero to a complete loser, or *vice versa*, in the space of 90 minutes. Only a select few players are above this kind of fickleness in Argentina. And it's even worse for the managers.

English players are given more respect by supporters, even if they have one or two poor games. Fans will still wait around after the match and ask politely for an autograph. This doesn't really happen in Argentina; the players are not so accommodating. In my opinion, the people's passion for football is equal in both countries. The noise levels at games are comparable – especially when we first came to England, even if Ossie and I had no idea what the crowd was actually chanting. A typical Argentine reaction to defeat, however, is a highly charged, emotional one. Fans will instinctively criticise their own players. In general, I think English fans assess a game in a more thoughtful manner. They're able to recognise that sometimes you have to accept that your team will be beaten by a better side, or lose to a great goal – there's no point in blaming anyone. They're more reasonable in their analysis. In that sense I found English supporters to be the more loyal of the two, which I really appreciated. The allegiance of an Argentine football fan is to his club, rather than to a specific player. As I see it, the way contracts are structured in each country is a factor here. Players sign much longer deals in England, whereas in Argentina they sign for just six months or a year. The people know these details, and this contributes to a heightened sense of loyalty in England; if you pledge your commitment to a club there, the fans respond in kind. It's easier to build a rapport that way. A few years ago I took my Argentine friend Ricardo Finocchiero to White Hart Lane to watch Tottenham play Newcastle United. Shortly before the end, by which time Spurs had the game sewn up, my friend looked across towards the corner of the ground where the Newcastle fans were gathered. They were still singing. Ricardo was confused. "I can't believe it," he said. "The game is lost.

Why are they behaving like this?" It was a new concept for him. But that's typical of English football supporters.

It's a big regret of mine that I was not able to find the success as a manager that would have vindicated my footballing philosophy. I just couldn't make it work. After leaving Defensa I failed to recapture the drive with which I operated throughout my first job as a manager. The energy and ambition that had engulfed me at Defensa gradually waned with each appointment. My dream of building the perfect attacking force just faded. I often found myself in dispute with club directors due to fundamental differences of opinion when it came to the game's basics. Targets at board level are purely results-driven, whereas I placed the onus on style. Winning was still the objective, of course. But winning with a flourish, in a positive, exciting manner, was always my ideal. Getting the spectators out of their seats was a priority. Give them value for money, I reasoned.

I know that Ossie had a similar experience when he was manager of Spurs. He was criticised for playing too many forwards – the 'Famous Five' led by Klinsmann and Sheringham – while supposedly neglecting the defensive side of the game. Steve Perryman, incidentally, enjoys telling a joke in relation to this. Steve was Ossie's assistant at Tottenham. He says that at training Ossie would gather in front of him the whole squad of, say, 25 players. "All the attacking players go to the left – you will be working with me today," he would say. "The other two will be doing some defensive work with Steve." In all seriousness, though, no manager would be so irresponsible. Ossie would never instruct his team to attack with eight players and leave three to defend. He just strongly believed in his principles and was desperate to treat the supporters. After all, it is possible. The Brazil team that won the World Cup in 1970 was arguably the greatest side of all time. They played with five – albeit exceptional – traditional number 10s.

I refrained from naming five forwards in any of the teams I managed. My favoured system was 4-3-1-2. At the back four defenders – as opposed to three – covered the whole width of the pitch. That gave the side a solid, ordered base. In front of them I had three midfielders, with one of them handed a specific holding role to protect the back four. In theory, my team would have at least seven players defending when the opposition were in possession. That should always be enough – how often will a team throw more than seven players into an attack? Up front, my two strikers – always two strikers – were instructed to play in between the lines of each post. In other words, they were told to stay central. That way, the fullbacks or midfielders were left with plenty of space down the flanks in which to advance. And when those wide men delivered crosses into the box there would – again, in theory – always be two centre forwards waiting to profit. Behind the front two I deployed a number 10, who assumed the free role in which I had felt most comfortable as a player. By definition these players are gifted, often maverick types whose responsibility it is to unlock opposing defences and create decisive openings. That mercurial flair is sometimes coupled with a reluctance to engage in the physical side of the game – the traditional number 10 is not the hardest working player on the pitch. The position is largely reliant on others providing *el número diez* with the ball. In possession, the team's orchestrator comes alive. Just like César Luis Menotti did with me, I allowed these flair players certain concessions. It's difficult to be brilliantly inventive in every match. Practically impossible in fact. Even Lionel Messi has quiet days. So whenever I had a player of that ilk under my reign I urged him to be positive. Menotti's words always filled me with confidence. He encouraged me to take players on and I did the same with my attacking players. "Play naturally," I told them. If they were in the team to create then I challenged them to do that, even if it didn't always come off. The potential rewards were worth persevering for.

Whatever system or style you implement as a manager, it is imperative that you genuinely believe in it. Some opt for more physical football than others. I wanted my players to express themselves. I couldn't be in control of a team that played like José Mourinho's Inter Milan did in winning the Champions League, for instance. That's not meant as a criticism. How can I knock José Mourinho? The man has achieved everything as a manager. Mourinho is a winner. Take the Champions League final against Bayern Munich for example. Bayern were in possession of the ball for long periods of the game but Inter were so formidable defensively, so economical and calculated in their approach. They were crowned European champions so it's difficult to argue with the manner in which they claimed that title as well as both domestic honours in Italy. I'm just a bit of a romantic when it comes to football I suppose. That's why I was sad when Inter knocked out the free-flowing Barcelona of Messi, Xavi and Iniesta in the semi-final. I'm not about to change my ideology though. Passing football can be winning football. Barcelona have shown that time and again in recent seasons.

Despite feeling disillusioned as a manager I wasn't ready to cut my ties with football. Early on in 2002 I was on holiday in England. I was at Ossie's house actually, when I received an unexpected phone call from an unexpected source – César Luis Menotti. My former national team boss was about to be named manager of Rosario Central, a club based north of Buenos Aires in the province of Santa Fe. His task was to drag the team out of a slump, and to do that he wanted to assemble a reliable team around him that would provide the club with a firm foundation from which they could progress. "The club is in a bad way," he informed me. "I need people here I can trust." My response was instant. "Of course," I said. *El Flaco* is my mentor, the most influential man in my footballing life. I loved working under him. The high esteem in which I held Menotti throughout the time I spent playing in his team never waned. Here was a chance to work with the great man once again, and I wasn't about to let it pass me by. I became youth team director at Rosario, overseeing events in all the junior divisions. It was a really enjoyable time for me. I ate lunch with Menotti every day. It was fascinating listening to him express his opinions on the game, imparting his extensive knowledge to the most receptive of audiences. We talked about football for hours. My stay at Rosario was short-lived, though. Just three or four months to be precise. As for the way in which my exit was fashioned, that led to one of the most terrifying experiences of my life and still makes me feel uncomfortable now. And it was all Ossie's fault!

Ossie rang me while I was in Rosario to tell me he'd accepted an offer to take charge of my old team Racing Club of Buenos Aires. "Come and join me," he said. I was tempted; the draw of a return to one of Argentina's 'Big Five' alongside my old sidekick was obvious. It was a fantastic opportunity for me to sample life at the sharp end of Argentinian football once more. "I like the sound of it," I replied. "Good," said Ossie. "Because I've already told everyone you're coming."

What?! "Hang on a minute," I countered. "It's not quite that simple." It was too late. Before I knew it there were television reports announcing that I'd left Rosario for Racing. All of a sudden I was stranded in the eye of a storm. Needless to say, the story was not well received in Rosario.

Menotti came to see me straight away. As you would expect, he wanted to know what was going on. I was in such an awkward position. I told him that I was considering Ossie's offer to assist him at Racing and that nothing had been finalised, even though media reports – and Ossie – had suggested otherwise. After a little deliberation I decided to stay in Rosario. Menotti had shown great faith in me and I felt I owed it to him to stick around. But Ossie eventually persuaded me to change my mind and in the end I did leave; 24 years after first-teaming up with Ossie at club level to embark on our great English adventure, we were back in tandem again. Menotti accepted my decision. Ossie and I went to his house in Buenos Aires and discussed the whole situation between us. Menotti knew it was a good opportunity for me and, typically, didn't stand in my way. He gave me his blessing and I left for Racing.

Problem solved? Not quite. Not at all, actually. After winning the opening game of the season away to Huracán, Racing then drew one and lost two of the next three games. One point from three matches constitutes something of a crisis in Argentina. Especially at a club of Racing's stature, and especially when the last of those three games was a 4-1 thrashing at the hands of arch rivals Independiente. The management, and Ossie in particular, were under pressure.

In our next game I inadvertently managed to take the focus of that pressure away from Ossie. I'd like to say it was because of a selfless act designed to take the heat off my pal at a difficult time. But it wasn't. We played Rosario Central at their *Gigante de Arroyito* stadium, where my controversial departure to Racing had made me public enemy number one. A joyful homecoming parade this was not. On the contrary, never in my life have I been so insulted.

Moving from a position of youth team director at one club to assistant manager at another is a switch that, under normal circumstances, barely registers with most football fans. This was different though. Because I was – erroneously – reported to have joined Racing without telling anyone at Rosario first I was cast as the villain of the piece. I'm convinced that the majority of Rosario fans didn't even know I was employed by their club until the overblown press coverage portrayed me as a traitor, triggering an explosion of anger.

What a day that was in Rosario. There is only way to get to the dugouts at Rosario's ground, by walking across the pitch from the dressing-rooms. That was the longest walk of my life. I was accompanied by police with riot shields to protect me from the various missiles being launched in my direction. What they couldn't stop, however, was the verbal onslaught that I was subjected to. "Villa, you son of a bitch! . . . We're going to kill you! . . . Traitor! . . . Judas! . . . You money-grabbing ****." It was awful. Awful for me, that is. For the Racing players around me it was the source of much amusement, watching me hastily stroll across the field whilst insults came firing in from all corners of the arena. "We didn't realise you were so popular here," they giggled. They thought the whole thing was hilarious. "I must remember to thank Ossie for this," I thought. I've a feeling that he quite enjoyed the whole episode too. At least it meant he was out of the spotlight that day. He'd actually been getting a bit of stick himself from opposing fans before that because of his reaction to a goal that Racing scored against Huracán on the opening day. He was caught on camera screaming "YES!" in English rather than expressing his delight in Spanish. Cue much mocking among rival supporters and accusations that Ossie was not Argentinian after all, but an Englishman instead.

I sat on the bench and didn't dare stick my head out of the dugout for the entire 90 minutes. To make matters worse we lost the match 4-0. In contrast to our stuttering form Rosario had started the season really well. With a vociferous full house behind them they took us apart. But that wasn't the end of the suffering for me. About one hour after the final whistle we left the ground to get on the team coach. Having been targeted by furious home fans from the moment I arrived at the stadium I was well aware that a final not-so-fond farewell may be in store as I boarded the bus. I've got to say, those crazy, unforgiving Rosario fans didn't let me down. As I emerged from the doorway a guy just a few yards away from me shouted, "Villa! Hijo de mil putas!" In English? "Villa! You son of a thousand whores!" Charming. He wasn't finished there, though. As I turned to face him – an instinctive reaction – he swung for me, launching a wild punch that I just about managed to evade. I wasn't expecting that.

I didn't want to fight the man, or any other irate Rosario supporter for that matter. Ideally, I would have sat them all down and explained that the media reports were in fact inaccurate, and that I hadn't agreed to leave Rosario without first informing the club of my decision. The situation is actually all my good friend's doing, I would have told them. If you're desperate to abuse someone then feel free to hurl a few insults Ossie's way, I felt like suggesting. You've got the wrong man. It was all Ossie's fault!

I survived that scary personal ordeal in Rosario, but there was still a much bigger issue that needed to be addressed. That resounding defeat, Racing's third on the trot, left us in a precarious position. Off the back of a derby-day hammering against Independiente – a game played at *el Monumental* because fan disturbances had led to Racing being banned from playing the match in their home stadium – the team performed badly in Rosario. Really badly. Myself, Ossie and the third member of our management team Emilio Commisso got together over dinner to thrash out a revival plan.

Ossie feared the worst, suggesting we were about to be axed. I disagreed. "We're in the danger zone, for sure, but the sack is not imminent," I stressed. We just need to make changes. Right away. "Who can we trust with our jobs?" we asked ourselves. Our futures were in the hands of the players. The three of us decided there and then that youth was the only way forward. Out with the old and in with the new. There was a vote between us regarding which players should be in the team, with Ossie having the deciding say. A group of youngsters were introduced, we urged them to be positive and thankfully the shake-up had the desired effect. From that moment on the team began to acquire its own identity as a slick, attacking side.

Racing won three of their next four league games, including a memorable 4-3 victory away to Boca Juniors in which Carlos Tévez was among the Boca goalscorers. The Racing winner that day was scored by Mariano González, a young player we'd thrown into the side as part of our emergency rebuilding exercise. His future clubs would include Inter Milan and Porto.

Another of the promising new brigade was a 23-year-old striker called Diego Milito. Despite his rawness the young Milito had an obvious eye for goal, as he has since demonstrated in Spain, with Real Zaragoza, and in Italy with Genoa and Inter Milan. Diego was far from the finished article when we had him at Racing, it has to be said. He would often concede possession too easily and needed several chances before scoring. What he did have, though, was a tremendous willingness to improve. He was a great professional and I saw for myself a significant improvement in the player thanks to the time that Ossie invested in him on the training pitch. I did wonder if he might struggle at Inter because signing for the Italian giants represented a huge step up for him. But José Mourinho gave him the necessary support, making him feel important, and Diego responded with 30 goals in Inter's treble-winning season of 2009/10 including two in their Champions League final victory over Bayern Munich. He deserves every plaudit he gets.

Racing recovered from a dreadful start to finish sixth in the opening stage of the season, the *Apertura* (two titles are contested in Argentina each year; the *Apertura*, which runs from August to December, and then – from February to June – the *Clausura*. Directly translated, *apertura* means opening, while *clausura* means closing). We took that momentum into the *Clausura*, remaining unbeaten in the first half-a-dozen games and topping the table early on before dropping off the pace later in the campaign. The team also did well in the Copa Libertadores, South America's version of the Champions League, going out to América de Cali on penalties at the last 16 stage despite not losing a single game in the competition. I felt that the team really improved under Ossie's guidance. Unfortunately he always maintained that if Racing didn't win anything he would leave at the end of the season. And that's what he did. Despite promising spells both domestically and in the Copa Libertadores Racing finished the 2002/03 campaign empty-handed. Our stay at the Avellaneda club was over.

I'm glad I spent that time working with Ossie. It was a great experience. The best thing for a manager is to know that his assistant has his back covered and Ossie definitely had that with me. Having been the boss at four clubs I did find it strange being a deputy at first. I soon adapted to the role, though. I got to know how Ossie liked to set his team up and how he operated in general. It didn't take me long to find my place in the management structure.

Being close friends obviously helped, as did the fact that our philosophies on how the game should be played were very similar. I was allowed to have my say and my opinion was respected. It was good fun, experiencing once again the drama and excitement that comes with working at a big club. The big crowds, the big games, the big victories. We talked about football every day, discussing all aspects of the game from players to opponents to dealing with the press. I loved the day-to-day involvement. I was impressed with the way in which Ossie combined English and Argentinian methods in training. He created a positive environment and I could see the players improving technically all the time, growing as a team. I honestly believe that Ossie did a perfect job at Racing. I'm grateful to have had the opportunity to work alongside him in the dugout. Even if it did make me the most unpopular man in Rosario.

Chapter Nineteen
EL CONCEJAL

Politics may not be the most popular pastime for many footballers, either past or present, but I've developed a real interest in the subject in my adult years. The origins of that interest can be traced back to various events that have occurred during my lifetime. Raúl Alfonsín's appointment as the first democratically elected president of Argentina following the military dictatorship in 1983, for instance, was one such event. The regime that preceded his term in office had been responsible for such brutality that the country was in a real mess in the early 1980s. Economically we were in a state of crisis, the Falklands War had been lost and thousands of civilians had disappeared as the junta sought to erase anyone who might oppose their rule or offer some sort of threat. It was a reign of terror, an unmitigated disaster. Alfonsín's arrival heralded a new start for Argentina. I was really impressed with the guy and I enjoyed listening to his speeches. He was a reasonable man, who immediately set about healing the wounds left by the previous regime. Alfonsín made mistakes, just as we all do. What he also did though was restore a state of calm to the country. He pacified the nation and helped unite the people. He also established a democracy that has existed in Argentina ever since – without any military inter-vention – and I believe we should all be grateful for that.

On closer reflection, though, I think my interest in politics dates back much further than that. All the way back, in fact, to 18th August 1952 – the date of my birth. I was born with a hostility towards authority, a sense of injustice if you like, and I've been acting on those impulses ever since. In that respect, my political persuasion is governed by instinct I suppose. I can vividly remember how, as a family, we strug-gled to deal with the economic situation when I was a child. My father rented a plot of land and we all worked hard around the farm just to make sure we could meet the payments. Every now and then that merciless man in a suit representing the landowners would appear to collect the rent, regardless of our circumstances; he didn't care if the weather had affected our crop, or if our livestock had been ravaged by disease. He just wanted his money.

The system seemed so unfair. How could we ever progress? The whole family mucked in every day just to keep our heads above water. I would always be a *peón*, I thought, unless I could find an alternative way out. Football offered that escape route of course, and my determination to succeed in that field was, to a large extent, borne out of the frustration created by our plight. I wanted to be free of the repression.

Even in my infancy I could see that the situation was unrea-sonable. Every man should have the chance to progress, but the system did not allow for that. There was no way out for the poorer people, who were by no means lazy. Far from it. The lower classes were extremely dedicated workers. They just weren't rewarded for their efforts, and weren't afforded the same opportunities as others when it came to things like education.

Everyone has their own beliefs and opinions, and one of mine is that there should be a more just redistribution of wealth. I am not a rich man – I played football in the wrong era for that to be the case. So some may feel it is easy for me to take such a stance. But I think the more affluent members of society have a duty to pay higher taxes and spread their riches to allow others to live with the dignity they deserve. Take Tiger Woods, for example. I'm a keen golfer myself, so I have complete respect for what he's achieved in the game. But I've read that the man is supposedly worth about $1 billion. How much money does a single person need? I know that a career at the top in any sport is relatively short-lived, and that Tiger Woods is a supremely gifted individual whose skill and application over the years has to be applauded. Surely you have to draw the line somewhere, though. It's almost obscene. I would feel uncomfortable if I earned that much money yet found myself surrounded by poverty. I honestly believe I would.

This is a debate that will rage on for ever, I know that. I would just like to see us address the needs of the poorer people in society. We should provide them with an education more than anything else. Simply handing out benefits, as some governments do, is not the answer. That can act as an incentive not to work, for those who are happy to pick up 200 pesos each month for doing nothing in return. By educating people, they have a chance to help themselves. Otherwise, they slave away all their lives for a pittance, retire, can't work any more and have nothing to live on. I find that very sad. Maybe this is a little too idealistic, but I believe quite strongly that society has to show a certain solidarity between its people right across the classes, and not just exploit those who are most vulnerable. There has to be a degree of mercy shown to the lower classes. A political representative, perhaps, who one can go to and say, "We've not had a good harvest" – for whatever reason – in the knowledge that they'll get a fair response. Not just "I don't care; pay up or you'll have to move on." As I mentioned earlier, my views and beliefs stem very much from my own experiences as a child.

Inspired by *Unión Cívica Radical* leader Raúl Alfonsín, I became a member of the Radical Party in 1983 when I returned to Roque Pérez after leaving Spurs. The *Unión Cívica Radical* was founded more than 100 years ago, and has existed throughout all the political turmoil that has plagued Argentina in that time. It was not until 1990, however, that I was able to take a more active role in politics. That was the year I settled back into my home town. Establishing a permanent base there enabled me to make a commitment that, due to the nomadic nature of my football career, had been impossible up to that point. My first step into the world of politics saw me stand to be a *concejal*. A *concejal* is like a councillor, of which there are ten in Roque Pérez serving under the mayor. A neighbour of mine, who was also a member of the Radical Party, encouraged me to go for the position. "Why not?" I thought. As part of the election campaign each candidate had to make a speech in the local park, which was a nerve-wracking ordeal. Playing football in front of 100,000 people? I could deal with that. Out on the pitch was where I felt most comfortable. That was my sort of arena. But delivering a political address before a few hundred local residents – now that was stressful. A real challenge. I managed to string a few words together and somehow I got elected! If I'm honest I think that my status as a former footballer helped me win a few votes. It's not an obvious correlation, but people seemed to think that because I was a decent player then maybe I would make a decent politician. Or perhaps they just liked the idea of having a famous *fútbolista* on the council. Either way, many locals knew me, or knew of me, and by assuming a position on the committee I could officially consider myself a politician.

People have never really seen past the fact that I was a footballer. It's often the first thing I'm asked about in interviews on TV or in newspapers. I can understand that – there aren't many of us who attempt to make the transition from footballer to politician. I'm aware of the novelty factor. That's not a problem, though, because it's generally accepted that I have political views and that I'm trying to make a difference. I believe that politics can change things in a big way in a small town like Roque Pérez.

There is an oligarchy of wealthy families who own vast areas of Roque Pérez and its surrounding region. Their monopoly was established many years ago by their Spanish forefathers and has continued through several generations. These people make huge sums of money from the land. I don't know them personally. I imagine they live in lavish houses elsewhere, probably in Buenos Aires, so we don't mix with them in the town. Like those wealthy landowners I have an historic association with Roque Pérez. Unlike them, however, the Villa family has never been part of the elite. Ours is a more traditional, working-class farming family. And this is where many journalists I have come into contact with have got it wrong. They assume that because I played football I must be rich, and that my politics err in favour of the wealthy. That's not the case at all. Money is important to me of course, but not that important. I've always taken it as it comes. Football has afforded me a certain lifestyle, I appreciate that. I never wanted to be rich, though, living a luxurious life in palatial surroundings while poverty was all around me. I would say my living status is comfortable. I'm neither rich nor poor. I certainly don't stand out and that is quite deliberate. I would never show off the little wealth that I have because I'm sensitive to the feelings of those around me who aren't able to live so comfortably. Sometimes I leave old shoes outside my house for others to pick up. It's not much, I know. I just wish they were brand new.

Until recently I was president of the Radical Party in Roque Pérez, where there are around 1,100 Radical Party members. That's a healthy number, especially when you consider how Fernando De La Rúa's troubled spell as leader – and president of Argentina – left many people disillusioned with the party. De La Rúa was the first *Unión Cívica Radical* president since Alfonsín. No one can deny that De La Rúa's reign, which began in 1999 and ended amid a series of riots in 2001, was unsuccessful. It was an economic catastrophe that led to Argentina defaulting on its debt. In contrast, the previous UCR president of Argentina Alfonsín is well regarded for the progress made during his tenure – even if respect for his efforts was a little late in coming. Only when he died, in 2009, did I sense that the Argentine public fully appreciated the significance of Alfonsín's work. In the aftermath of the harsh military junta Alfonsín kept the country relatively peaceful. He united us behind the flag. Call me a cynic but I wasn't so sure that the changes he instigated would ever be duly recognised. I'm glad to admit I was wrong on that count though, with a sizeable crowd attending his funeral and newspaper tributes and obituaries all carrying a positive theme. So there is hope for the Radical Party. My good friend Ricardo Alfonsín – the son of Raul – recently launched his bid to become the UCR's national leader and I travelled to Córdoba to lend him my support. I wouldn't say that I have any major political ambitions now, but I do remain firmly behind Ricardo and the party.

In terms of social climate and politics Roque Pérez is typically Argentinian. As a country, we govern looking backwards rather than forwards. Instead of concentrating their focus on the future, anyone assuming a political position here must first tackle the problems left behind by the previous incumbent. That's why political leaders, mayors and presidents are constantly clashing with their predecessors. This is wrong of course. We should be thinking ahead, formulating long-term plans and goals to make improvements in areas like healthcare, education, security – although crime is less of a problem in towns like Roque Pérez than it is in the big cities – and traffic congestion. This would enable people to live more progressive lives.

I would like to see our residents become more involved in these issues. There is a tendency here, as there is right across the country – and probably across many other countries too – for folk to get on with their own lives without much care for the progression of their neighbours. I wish they would embrace politics a little more by getting involved and having their say, rather than simply criticising their local representatives and voicing their disapproval. Without the involvement of the people politicians cannot make effective changes, so I urge the whole community to play a part. I think a more collective mentality has to be adopted. That's my ideal. I was fortunate in that my career took me all over the world. I saw many different countries and experienced many different cultures. I realise that we need to pay more attention to the issues I've just mentioned – healthcare, education, policing and so on – in order to make things more comfortable for the inhabitants of my town.

The current social dynamic in Roque Pérez is an interesting one that forms a topic of much debate. There are just over 10,000 people living in the town and, in theory, there is little unemployment. The situation is a bit more detailed than that, though, because many of those who do work are without a permanent salary. To explain why that is, one has to understand that Roque Pérez is entirely dependent on the farming industry. Labourers are employed at different points of the year, such as at harvest time, with some travelling great distances to work here. They come from some of the poorest provinces in the north of Argentina, like Santiago Del Estero and el Chaco. The situation suits both parties – it's cheap labour for the farmers, while the workers get accommodation (usually a modest hut), food and a wage (albeit a minimal one). The labourers come with the intention of working in Roque Pérez for the harvest period alone, but what tends to happen is that they often find the arrangement to their liking. Instead of returning north once their initial term ends they stay put. This is how the population of Roque Pérez has grown. Personally, I don't have a problem with this.

Troubles exist all over Argentina, one of which is widespread poverty. The issue of poverty is a prime concern. How can we have such poverty in a country that also boasts extreme wealth? It frustrates me. Some feel that if we don't address the problem then one day the poor could turn against those in power. This would be disastrous. What if 5–10,000 poor people were to rise up and rebel against 1,000 or so members of the middle class, who – it must be said – don't work any harder than the poorer sector of society? We may not be far away from that kind of civil unrest.

I think we have to show solidarity as a nation and help those who are underprivileged. Why shouldn't the municipality help the labourers settle by housing them? I welcome them. As I've already said, Roque Pérez is totally reliant on the farming trade. It drives the whole economy of the town and the labourers are at the heart of that. They work hard. We shift vast amounts of grain and cattle in Roque Pérez and the money generated by selling those products trickles down the social scale to afford all of us a more dignified way of life. Like most topics on the political agenda this one is far from straightforward. I realise that. Sometimes the settlers, impressed by the way in which they are treated in their new home, invite their cousins and other family members to join them. Locals get annoyed when they see 'outsiders' given priority when it comes to benefits and housing, hence the sensitivity surrounding the subject and the difference of opinion it provokes. Either way, our number is growing and we must have the necessary infrastructure in place to deal with that.

So there you have it. Political rant over! I served a four-year term as a *concejal*, during which time I acted as a representative of the local community, trying to make sure that public services met their needs and that any issues of concern – such as housing – were dealt with. I tried, as best I could, to help establish some progression and in some areas it worked. One initiative we introduced, for example, was a training course for local nurses. The move was a big success, with the hospital in Roque Pérez taking on a stream of well-educated, professional staff. I enjoyed my time as an active politician. I delivered speeches in the park and I drove around the town voicing my policies through a loudspeaker at election time. I've chaired meetings and presided over political conventions. Even though I didn't achieve everything I set out to do, or make all the changes I intended to, I kept striving towards those goals. Just as I did as a footballer.

Chapter Twenty

AND STILL RICKY VILLA...

The singer Robbie Williams reminded me a few years ago of the place that I seem to occupy in the consciousness of England's footballing public. This, it has to be said, never ceases to amaze me. Robbie Williams, as far as I'm aware, doesn't speak Spanish. So, when he was on stage at River Plate's *el Monumental* stadium in front of 60,000 or so hysterical fans – they love him here in Buenos Aires – he decided upon an alternative way of connecting with his audience. Due to his limited grasp of the local language he opted for the next best thing, namely to shout out a name that he was sure the crowd would be familiar with, in the hope of provoking a positive response. "RICKY VILLA!!!" he screamed, right in the middle of his performance.

People in England still remember me because of a goal I scored some 30 years ago, and I find that incredible. Wonderful, but incredible. And it's not just famous pop stars who are doing their bit to keep the memory of 1981 alive. A friend in England told me that he was watching *Match of the Day* recently when a Stoke player scored a goal by dribbling around a few defenders and sweeping the ball past the goalkeeper. Whilst analysing the mazy run and finish on that evening's programme, the presenter Gary Lineker said, "That was just like Ricky Villa." It's astonishing really. Three decades on from my 'moment' and people are still referring to it.

I visit England each year, and I have to say that I feel more integrated there now than ever before. At first, settling in London was hard. It wasn't easy for a foreigner living so far away from home in 1978. If I had joined a club in almost any other European country I wouldn't have lasted two weeks. But the cordiality of the English people was such that I felt compelled to give it a go. Their support inspired me to do at least that. It's the same whenever I go back to England now. After leaving Spurs in 1983 I didn't return until the 1987 FA Cup final. I was given a decent reception at Wembley that day, although it was nothing like the one I received when I was introduced to the White Hart Lane crowd at half-time of a game against Newcastle United shortly after the turn of the millennium. The supporters went crazy when I walked onto the pitch. I was looking all around the ground wondering, "Is this all for me?" It was really quite moving.

Now I always visit White Hart Lane when I'm back in England. I love those visits. In fact, I've made almost as many appearances at the ground since leaving as when I was a player there! The crowd sing my name and it thrills me every time. In 2008 Ossie and I were both inducted into the Tottenham Hotspur Hall of Fame. The truth is I don't feel worthy of a place in it. It's an overwhelming privilege. Some players have made hundreds of appearances for Spurs – many more than the 179 that I made – but have yet to receive Hall of Fame recognition. Ossie had a much longer, more productive Tottenham career than me, but I am in there next to him and the rest of the club's finest. There's still no separating the two of us.

I had no idea of the legacy I'd left at Tottenham when I departed the club almost unnoticed in 1983. I didn't appreciate how one goal could guarantee me such a prominent place in the club's history. That history is illuminated by great, great players like Danny Blanchflower and Jimmy Greaves, and I'm immensely proud to feature alongside them in the Tottenham Hotspur story.

Despite enduring a difficult start to life at White Hart Lane I look back on my career without any regrets. I wouldn't swap my Tottenham experience for anything. England taught me so many things. Discipline, for one. In Argentina, if you were asked to be somewhere at two o'clock it was regarded as a loose approximation. Maybe you would turn up at half past two, or three o'clock. In England, two o'clock meant two o'clock. I discovered that football in England was so professional in every aspect. We never lacked for proper food, medical attention or training equipment, for example. For me, this – along with the honesty that exists within the game and a proud history dating back more than 100 years – is what makes the English league one of the best and most prestigious leagues in the world.

Everyone connected with football in England has total respect for the history of the game. I became aware of that on one particular afternoon, quite soon after I'd arrived in the country. Shortly before kick-off in one of my earliest games for Spurs – away to Norwich – the stadium announcer stood by the pitch and addressed the crowd. I looked over and asked a teammate if he knew what was happening. I was told that a presentation was about to be made to Martin Peters, one of England's 1966 World Cup winners. When he stepped forward and acknowledged the supporters every single spectator rose to their feet and applauded. It was a wonderful reaction. It was such a respectful gesture that the moment really left a mark on me. From that point on I began to understand English football, and how the fans appreciated the game's background. Ossie and I were told all about Bill Nicholson and Tottenham's great past, the double-winning side of 1961 and so on. It was all part of our education.

As for Wembley, that looks a little bit different now from when I played at the famous old arena. In 2007, I was invited back there to attend the first FA Cup final at the refurbished stadium. I was paraded on the pitch alongside Steve Perryman and several other former FA Cup winners as part of the official opening ceremony. Call me old-fashioned, but despite being a magnificent stadium it doesn't quite feel like Wembley to me any more. The twin towers were such a powerful, historic symbol of the old ground. I was sad when they knocked them down.

As much as I enjoy returning to England it was never my intention to settle there like Ossie has. Ossie and his family still live near London and that is their home now. The boys have grown up and have families of their own, so the Ardiles roots are planted firmly in English soil. For me, the long-term plan was always to live in Argentina. I missed my country when I was away – the people, the customs, the climate. Roque Pérez is my home. It's where I grew up. It's where my family and oldest friends are. It's where I feel completely at ease.

Each person goes through life along their chosen path. We all make decisions according to our ambitions, or based on what we enjoy doing. I always had a clear ideal in my mind. That ideal was to be living in Roque Pérez, enjoying the fruits of my small achievements in life surrounded by my loved ones. It's not the most conventional of plans for a retired footballer – I don't think any of my former teammates who came from small towns have gone back to live there. They prefer more affluent locations offered by the big cities. City life is not for me. Sometimes Cristina and I travel into Buenos Aires – the drive only takes an hour or so – and on arriving back home afterwards we sit in our garden drinking *mate* and reflect on how lucky we are, with our happy, tranquil existence. All the hustle and bustle of the city is not for us. Besides, where could you ride a horse in Buenos Aires?! Give me a quiet rural outpost any day.

I have Argentinian friends in England who questioned my decision to go home. But I love my life in Roque Pérez and I couldn't imagine living apart from my family and friends. My father – my great friend – passed away in 1996 but my mother lives with us in a detached living area at the back of our house. My sister Noemí and her husband Chacho are still in the town. Cristina's Aunt Rosita, who accompanied us to England in 1978 and shared with us that strange experience of landing in a foreign country for the first time, pops in most days. And, last but by no means least, the little ray of sunshine that is our beautiful granddaughter Julia regularly illuminates our house with her presence.

Our four children, Maru, Martina, Mariana and Ricky (there isn't "only one Ricky Villa" after all!) are all based in Buenos Aires. They live together in a flat we bought, although they spend most weekends back home with us. That's a familiar trend in the town, with the children of local families studying and working in the city but returning home each Friday night. It's nice, our kids meet up with their friends and there's a constant stream of people coming in and out of our house every Saturday and Sunday. I like that. It makes for a close-knit environment and helps create a strong community spirit.

I'm proud that all four of our children are university-educated. It was always a priority of mine to give my kids an opportunity to study at that level. It was a chance that I never had when I was younger and it gave me great satisfaction to see them progress academically. Maru has a degree in political science and now works in local government; Martina is a doctor, specialising in gynaecology; Mariana is a psychologist; and Ricky is currently studying agricultural engineering.

As for my old sidekick Ossie, we're still the best of friends. That doesn't mean we contact each other all the time, though. Ossie likes to e-mail rather than talk, and I like to talk rather than e-mail. Not the best foundations for a regular stream of communication! Whenever I visit England, I always stay at Ossie's house, where he, Sylvia and the rest of the wonderfully hospitable Ardiles family ensure that every trip is an enjoyable one. It's my favourite hotel in the world! I also take the opportunity to catch up with many other old friends. Golf is ideal in that respect – it's such a social activity. Although I must admit I struggle a bit when I play with Pat Jennings; with his softly spoken voice and strong Irish accent I can't understand a word he says! Mind you, he probably says the same about me.

I still come into contact with a number of Spurs fans as well. Whenever I'm back in England I take part in 'An Evening with . . . ' events, which involve me taking to the stage alongside the likes of Ossie and Steve Perryman, speaking in front of an audience and taking questions from the floor. Everyone has a few drinks and a comedian provides further entertainment, then we sign a few autographs afterwards. They're always good nights. It's wonderful to see so many Tottenham supporters retaining such a fondness for our era.

I get recognised more often when I'm in England than when I'm in Argentina. Maybe the fact that I'm still sporting a distinctive beard helps, even if it has greyed over the years. I was probably still a teenager when I first grew it. To be honest, it felt really uncomfortable back then. But its appearance seemed to coincide with my early progression as a footballer so I thought I'd keep it for good luck. It's stayed ever since, although I have shaved it off to mark special occasions in my life – when I won the World Cup, when I won the FA Cup, when my first child was born. It was a kind of sacrificial gesture, I suppose. I kept a long moustache each time though; I didn't want to do anything too drastic!

Not so long ago I went to the bank in England and the girl at the counter asked me my name. When I told her she said, "Ricky Villa? You used to play for Tottenham!" and then someone behind me in the queue said, "I remember your goal!" The people never forget. On another recent visit I met Chris Hughton's parents. They told me they still had pictures of me from the Cup final on their wall at home. Incidents like these sum up the special way in which English people treasure their national game.

Looking back, football had an enormous say in my past. In the present, however, I'm outside of the game. I enjoy watching football on television, and I occasionally attend matches in Buenos Aires. As a former World Cup winner I have a pass that grants me access to any game in the country, so I sometimes exercise that luxury. I may have only made two substitute appearances in the whole of the tournament, but it doesn't say that on the pass! As far as football is concerned, though, I'm not directly connected with it any more. I miss certain aspects of it, for sure, but I don't crave that involvement like so many of my old friends do. Of course, from an egotistical point of view, I sometimes think it would be nice to be a manager again, but those thoughts never linger for too long.

And, even though my involvement in football is now minimal, it doesn't look like those who are still associated with the game are about to forget me. I was reminded of this when Tottenham played Manchester City in their penultimate Premier League match of the 2009/10 campaign. With both teams eyeing fourth place it was virtually a Champions League qualification play-off. A huge, huge game. Because of the two teams involved a *Daily Mail* reporter phoned me at my house in Roque Pérez to interview me ahead of the match. It's amazing that I'm still a point of reference on such occasions after all this time. Not that I'm complaining.

I watched the game at home on television as Tottenham won 1-0 to secure fourth place. During the match the commentator mentioned me, Ossie and the Cup final. Then when I visited England shortly after that I bumped into someone who was at the game in Manchester. He told me that Spurs took something like 3,000 fans to the game and at one stage they were teasing Manchester City supporters with chants of "One Ricky Villa, there's only one Ricky Villa . . ." Again, incredible. Another person I crossed paths with on that trip to England was Kevin Bond, Harry Redknapp's assistant at Spurs whose father John was manager of Manchester City in 1981. "My dad is still not happy with you!" he said. I told him to pass on my apologies. What else could I say?!

My day-to-day life now revolves around the farmland. From farmer to footballer to farmer again, that's me. Except that, as the landowner, I make all the decisions now. I have 350 hectares of land on which I grow soya that is harvested and sold once a year. I have 300 cows to keep under control too. That entails regular checks on their whereabouts and general health. I drive out along the dusty roads and across the fields in my jeep to inspect the stock. I check the condition of the surrounding fences that pen them in – carrying out any repairs if necessary – and I make sure they have an adequate supply of water. If I'm out in the field when one of the herd is giving birth then I help deliver the calf. I've also got about 20 sheep, three horses and a couple of dogs.

I'm completely content in Roque Pérez, a town that is an integral part of my identity. I feel I've been lucky. Lucky to have achieved my dream of playing football. Lucky that football took me all over the world and made me a more educated man in the process. Lucky to have a wonderful family around me. I'm home again now. My life has come full circle. I ride my horses across the same land as I did as a child and farm the same fields that my father used to farm. Once a *gaucho*, always a *gaucho*. My life no longer revolves around football. But I'll always have the memories. I don't need to keep reminding myself of past glories by watching recordings on video or DVD. My son occasionally puts the '81 Cup final on when his friends are at our house. I never join them in front of the television. I've got other things to do. Like stand in the doorway at the back of the room and discreetly glance at the screen from there instead. Just to make sure the little boy from *el campo* really did score the winning goal. And I still wonder how he ever made it as a *futbolista*.

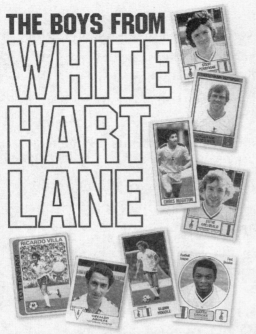

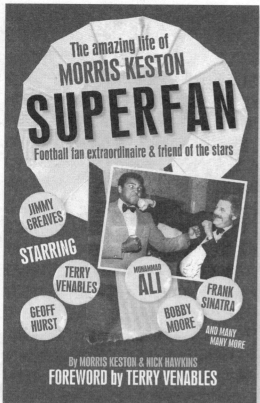

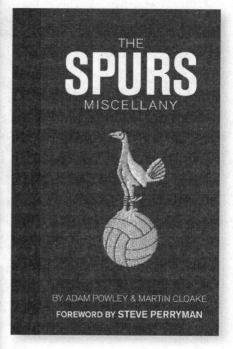